ermission to use material from this book please contact us:
hone 631-231-7269; Fax 631-231-8175
Site: http://www.novapublishers.com

dditional color graphics may be available in the e-book version of this book.

ibrary of Congress Cataloging-in-Publication Data

emand for money in developing countries : alternative estimates and policy implications / editor, aten Kumar.
pages cm. -- (Economic issues, problems and perspectives)
Includes bibliographical references and index.
ISBN: 978-1-62948-037-4 (softcover)
1. Demand for money--Developing countries. 2. Money supply--Developing countries. 3. Monetary policy--Developing countries. I. Kumar, Saten.
HG1496.D458 2014
339.5'3091724--dc23
2014011647

Published by Nova Science Publishers, Inc. † New York

ECONOMIC ISSUES, PROBLEMS AND PERSPECTIVES

DEMAND FOR MONEY IN DEVELOPING COUNTRIES

ALTERNATIVE ESTIMATES AND POLICY IMPLICATIONS

Economic Issues, Problems and Perspectives

Additional books in this series can be found on Nova's website under the Series tab.

Additional e-books in this series can be found on Nova's website under the e-book tab.

Demand for Money Developing Countr

Alternative Estimat and Policy Implicatio

Saten Kumar

New York

CONTENTS

PREFACE

This book offers insights on the stability of money demand for developing countries using more up-to-date econometric techniques and data. The demand for money is an important topic in monetary economics. The money demand stability is an empirical issue and given the importance of the topic, robust empirical results are required. The existing literature has focused largely on the advanced countries; however there has been a growing interest on this topic for developing countries. Analyzing the money demand functions allows us to evaluate the stance of monetary policy in terms of appropriateness of existing instruments or tools. A number of studies in the literature argue that most central banks of developing countries could still utilize the supply of money as an instrument of monetary policy. Controversy remains in the literature with the estimates of income elasticities and stability of the money demand. Regrettably, the existing literature does not offer guidelines on identifying strong empirical evidence given the multitude of econometric methods that are on offer. There exist contrasting views in relation to whether the central banks should use the rate of interest policy. It appears that most central banks pay less attention to the stability of the money demand functions; therefore this publication attempts to shed light on the usefulness of money demand stability for monetary policy.

Chapter 1

INTRODUCTION

The demand for money function is justifiably considered to be among the fundamental behavioral relationships in macroeconomics. A stable demand for money function is a necessary condition to use money supply as an instrument of monetary policy. Poole (1970) has argued that to minimize fluctuations in the level of economic activity, money supply should be used as an instrument when the liquidity money (*LM*) relation is stable and the rate of interest is the appropriate instrument when the *LM* relation is unstable. Since instability in the demand for money is a major factor contributing to instability in the *LM*, it is important to test for the stability of the money demand function for selecting the monetary policy instrument. Selecting the wrong instrument will cause more instability in output.

The switch from money supply to interest rate, as the monetary policy instrument, has taken place in the developed countries due to instability of their money demand functions. This was due to the financial innovations, following liberalization policies of the 1980's. However, many developing countries have also switched to using the bank rate as their monetary policy instrument although there is no evidence that their liberalization policies have had large enough effects to make their demand for money functions unstable. For instance, Rao and Singh (2005a and 2005c) found that demand for money functions in Fiji and India are stable. Similarly, Singh and Kumar (2010 and 2012) found that demand for money functions in 12 developing countries viz., Fiji, Vanuatu, Samoa, Solomon Islands, India, Indonesia, Philippines, Thailand, Kenya, Malawi, Jamaica and Rwanda are temporally stable. Nevertheless, if these countries switch to using the bank rate as their instrument of monetary policy, there would be more instability in economic activity.

The estimates of the demand for money are useful for understanding the limits to non-inflationary seignorage revenue and for the formulation of monetary policy targets. It is noted that empirical works on demand for money continues with renewed vigor, for several reasons, in spite of some well established stylized facts about income and interest rate elasticities. Most studies are based on the industrial countries, for example United States, United Kingdom and Australia and relatively fewer studies were carried out on developing countries. However the empirical studies on developing countries has been rising in the recent years because of the concern among researchers on the effects of flexible exchange rate regimes, globalization of capital markets, financial reforms and liberalization on the demand for money.

The theory suggests that the demand for money is a function of scale variable (income is widely used but at times industrial output is also used) and set of opportunity cost variables (mostly the nominal rate of interest on the treasury bills). Keynes criticized the quantity theorists for their assumption of a constant velocity and argued that velocity is affected by behavioural economic variables such as the nominal rate of interest. He argued that demand for money is negatively related to the nominal interest rate is a significant departure from the classical quantity theory of money demand. Alternatively, Friedman's theory of the demand for money does not deal with the motives for holding money. Friedman used theory of portfolio choice and argued that demand for money depends on permanent income and the incentives for holding other assets relative to money. Friedman concluded that the demand for money is stable and by and large insensitive to interest rates because relative rates seldom change.

However, in the empirical literature much of the controversy is for different reasons and on the relative merits of alternative time series techniques. While some prefer the systems based method of Johansen's maximum likelihood (JML), others are comfortable with the simpler single equation methods like the London School of Economics-Hendry's General to Specific (GETS) and the Phillip-Hansen's Fully Modified OLS (FMOLS) approaches.[1] Smith (2000) has pointed out, statistical techniques are only tools to summarize data and therefore they cannot answer difficult questions that need economic insights. According to Smith there are three stages in applied works viz., purpose, summary and interpretation. A similar view is also taken by Rao (2007). It is noted that often applied economists neglect the first and

[1] For an interesting methodological debate on the relative merits of alternative time series approaches, see discussion in Smith (2000).

third stages and pay too much attention to the econometric techniques. In this book, I show that alternative estimation methods give similar and consistent summaries of data if the theory is sound and data are reliable. Therefore, I take the view that while it is desirable to use a few alternative methods of estimation, adequate attention should also be paid to the purpose and the need for preparing alternative summaries and their interpretations.

In this book, I have used the money demand relationship to provide some empirical support for the aforesaid conjuncture. Three techniques (JML, GETS and FMOLS) have been employed to estimate the short and long run relationships between the demand for narrow money and its determinants for 15 developing countries. I have also used the Gregory and Hansen (1992) procedure to test for structural breaks in the money demand cointegrating equation. Our sample countries with acronyms in brackets are; Fiji (FJI), Vanuatu (VNT), Samoa (SAM), Solomon Islands (SOL), Tonga (TNG), India (IND), Indonesia (IDN), Philippines (PHL), Thailand (THA), Bangladesh (BGD), Kenya (KEN), Malawi (MWI), Jamaica (JAM), Rwanda (RWA) and South Africa (ZAF).

Having obtained the parameter estimates, I also examine if the income and interest rates elasticities differ significantly across these countries as some like India and Indonesia are very large with a large volume of transactions and others like Fiji, Samoa, Solomon Islands, Tonga and Vanuatu are small island countries. There are also medium sized countries like the Philippines, Thailand and Kenya. It would be interesting, therefore, to examine if the demand for money depends on the size of the country and the volume of transactions. This is of interest because, compared to the developed countries, cash is often used as the medium of exchange in the day to day transactions in many developing countries. Further, since the long- and short- run estimates are at hand, we also test if the money demand relations remain stable in light of the financial reforms in all these countries. This is important for policy because central banks in many developing countries have switched to interest rate as their policy instrument and abandoned targeting the money supply. This is partly due to trailing the advanced countries in targeting the rate of interest after the financial reforms.

The outline of this book is as follows. In Chapter 2, I examine the importance of demand for money. In Chapter 3 I survey some recent empirical studies on money demand in the industrial and developing countries. Chapter 4 is the empirical results and finally conclusions and limitations are given in Chapter 5.

Chapter 2

IMPORTANCE OF DEMAND FOR MONEY

2.1. INTRODUCTION

There is a vast amount of literature on demand for money on industrial and developing countries. Most of these studies ignored to explain the purpose of estimating demand for money. In this chapter I will discuss the importance of studying demand for money, with special reference to the baseline theories of demand for money. I also shed some light on monetary policy instruments and financial reforms.

This chapter is organized as follows: Sections 2 and 3, respectively, detail the theories of demand for money and the monetary policy targets and instruments. Section 4 briefly discusses the financial reforms and instability in the money demand functions and conclusions are stated in Section 5.

2.2. THEORIES OF DEMAND FOR MONEY

2.2.1. Classical Quantity Theory

The classical quantity theory explains the direct and proportional relationship between the quantity of money and the price level.[1] Irving Fisher's equation of exchange and the Cambridge approach are the two versions of the classical quantity theory. Both versions present the transactions demand for money, that is, money as a medium of exchange. Fisher introduced

---

[1] For a detailed discussion on the alternative theories of demand for money, see Serletis (2001).

the transactions version of the equation of exchange.[2] However, the income version of the equation of exchange (Equation 1 below) includes income velocity and assumes that real income and volume of transactions are proportionately related.

$$M^s V = PY \tag{1}$$

where M^s is the actual money supply, V is the velocity of circulation, P is the price level and Y is the real output. Fisher assumed that real activity and money are exogenously determined. That is, velocity has a constant equilibrium value and the price level is the only endogenous variable. Thus the Fisher equation is written as[3]

$$\bar{M}^s \bar{V} = \bar{P}\bar{Y} \tag{2}$$

Equation (2) states the conditions under which nominal income is determined solely by movements in the quantity of money. The quantity theory of money becomes a theory of demand for money when it is assumed that the money market is in equilibrium condition. The important thing to note here is that demand for money is solely a function of income. The rate of interest has no effect on the demand for money.

Similar to Fisher, the Cambridge economists assumed that real income is exogenous and demand for money is proportional to prices.[4] An additional assumption here is that money supply is exogenous and money is willingly held so that money demand equals money supply. The Cambridge cash balance equation implies that nominal income is determined by the quantity of money. Unlike the quantity theorists, the Cambridge economists allowed for the possibility of interest rate effects on the demand for money in the short run. This led Keynes to develop a theory of demand for money that emphasized the significance of interest rate and liquidity preference.

---

[2] Irving Fishers transactions version of the equation of exchange is $M^s\ V = PT$ where M^s is the actual money supply, V is the velocity of circulation, P is the price level and T is the volume of transactions.

[3] The bars indicate that the variables are independently determined.

[4] The Cambridge cash balance equation is $M^d = kPY$ where M^d is the demand for money, P is the price level and Y is the real income. They argued that money demand will be a constant fraction, k, of income.

2.2.2. Keynesian and Monetarist Debate

The Keynesian theory of demand for money or liquidity preference is a negative function of the interest rate. Keynes criticized the quantity theorists for their assumption of a constant velocity and argued that velocity is affected by behavioral economic variables. Keynes extended the Cambridge theory of money demand by analyzing not only the effects of changes in income on money demand, but the effect of changes in the interest rates and expectations of future changes in the interest rate on money demand. Money supply is assumed to be fixed by the central bank. From the equality of money demand and supply, the *LM* curve is derived as a positive function in interest rates, income space. A rise in income increases money demand, which requires a rise in the interest rate to restore equilibrium in the money market.

In the pure Keynesian case *LM* is horizontal and interest is perfectly elastic because everyone expects that the rate of interest has reached its lowest rate and it will increase in the future. Since holding bonds (the only alternative asset to holding money) will entail enormous capital losses, wealth holders forego return on bonds and hold cash that has no return. Whether monetary policy can stimulate the economy then depends on where *IS* intersects *LM* in the Keynesian flat zone of *LM*. Keynes believed that any change in the supply of money in the main would be offset by a change in velocity. Thus he regarded the quantity theory equation in its Cambridge cash balance version to be valid as an identity but useless for policy or for predicting short run fluctuations in income.

According to Keynes, liquidity preference is based on three motives. First, there is transactions motive where people hold cash balances in order to be able to make payments. Second, there is a precautionary motive where people hold cash balances for unexpected events or emergencies. Third, the speculative motive which takes into account the preferences for money holdings relative to other stores of wealth such as bonds.

Keynes did not regard the demand for money arising from transactions motive and precautionary motive as technically fixed in its relationship to the level of income, see Laidler (1977). The most important innovation in Keynes' analysis of the demand for money is his speculative demand for money. The primary result of the Keynesian speculative theory is that there is negative relationship between demand for money and interest rate. This result is derived by Keynes by analyzing the choice between interest yielding bonds and money as an issue of liquidity preference. Along these lines, Keynes raised the importance of variables such as interest rates, expectations and uncertainty in the theory of the demand for money.

Keynes postulated that when the rate of interest is expected to fall, the demand for money is relatively low, since people hold bonds in anticipation of capital gains. Alternatively, when the rate of interest is expected to rise, the demand for money is greater as people seek to avoid making capital losses on holding bonds. Keynes considered the current level of interest rate as an indicator of interest rate changes or expectations. This implies that the demand for speculative money balances, which is the largest component in the demand for money, depends on the nominal interest rate and people's expectation of future rates.

Further, Keynes argued that people's decision to hold bonds or money is in terms of some *normal value* of interest rates, see Serletis (2001). If interest rates are above this normal value, people will expect them to fall, bond prices to rise and capital gains would be realized. In this case people would be more willing to hold their liquid wealth as bonds rather than money and the demand for money would be low. On the other hand, if interest rates are below the normal value, people will expect them to rise, bond prices to fall and capital losses to be realized. People would be more willing to hold money than bonds and the demand for money would be high.

The three motives for holding money can be combined to get the Keynesian demand for money function or liquidity preference function:

$$(M / P) = f(Y, r) \tag{3}$$

The above equation serves to illustrate that the demand for money (M/P) is positively related to real income (Y) and negatively related to nominal interest rate (r). One implication of the Keynesian liquidity preference theory is that the velocity is not constant but positively related to nominal interest rates. It also implies that the velocity is procyclical since procyclical interest rate movements induce procyclical velocity movements.

Further, the speculative demand for money becomes discontinuous of its current level for an individual with expectations about the future level of interest rate, see Laidler (1977) for detailed discussion. Keynes argued that at some low level of interest rate everyone will expect the rate to rise and people would be unwilling to hold bonds and prefer holding money. Here the demand for money at aggregate level becomes perfectly elastic with respect to interest rates. The rate of interest will not change and any rise in quantity of money would leave interest rate unchanged. This is regarded as the liquidity trap, meaning that interest elasticity of money demand becomes infinity at low levels of rate of interest. The main implication is that monetary policy becomes ineffective and therefore fiscal policy is only means of economic control.

Keynesian analysis is based on the proposition that at any time there is a normal rate of interest. This normal rate of interest is constant overtime is something not regarded in Keynes analysis. However, the speculative demand for money depends on the current level of interest rate relative to this normal level. According to Laidler (1977), the model implies that the relationship between demand for money and the interest rate would be unstable overtime, therefore effectiveness of monetary policy and fiscal policy alike is impossible to assess on the basis of a model that treats this relationship as a stable one. The main Keynesian view is that the demand for money should be treated not as some special matter but rather as a particular application of the general theory of demand.

Monetarist Milton Friedman opposed the Keynesian view that money does not matter. Friedman (1956) presented the quantity theory as a theory of demand for money. Friedman assumes that money is abstract purchasing power, meaning that people hold it with intention of using it for upcoming purchases of goods and services, integrated as asset theory and a transactions theory of the demand for money within the context of neoclassical microeconomic theory of consumer and producer behaviour. To households money is one kind of asset, one way of holding wealth. To firms, money is a capital good that combined with other sources of productive services yields the products that firms sell. Friedman interprets the theory of demand for money as a special topic in the theory of capital, see Serletis (2001) for further discussion.

The demand for money by households, like their demand for other consumption services, is dependent on total human and non-human wealth (the budget restraint), the expected price of and return on money and alternative forms of wealth, as well as inter-temporal rates of substitution, tastes and preferences of household wealth holders. Friedman distinguishes between real and nominal magnitudes and casts the demand for money by households as a demand for real balances -- a function of real variables independent of nominal money values.

A firm's demand to hold more or less money, like their demand for other productive services, depends on the cost of the productive services money yields, the cost of substitute productive services and the value of the product the productive service yields. Like the household the firm's demand for money is a demand for real balances, responsive to rates of return on bonds, equities, and on other assets as well as the rate of change of the price level. From Friedman's viewpoint, the Keynesian distinction between "active balances and idle balances" and "transaction balances and speculative balances" is irrelevant. Each unit of money renders a variety of services that the household or firm equates at the margin.

Friedman's money demand function can be expressed for an individual wealth holder as follows:[5]

$$\left(M / P\right) = f\ \left(Y_p, R_b - R_m, R_e - R_m, \Pi^e - R_m, \ldots\right) \tag{4}$$

where Y_p is real permanent income, R_b is expected nominal rate of return on bonds, R_e is expected nominal rate of return on equities, R_m is expected nominal rate of return on money and Π^e is expected inflation rate. The dots in Equation (4) stand for other variables for example the ratio of human to non-human wealth which has no important implications for monetary policy. The expected nominal rate of return on bonds includes expected capital gains and losses and that on equities includes expected changes in prices. Further, the expected inflation rate is used as a proxy for expected nominal rate of return on physical assets.

Friedman argued that money matters a great deal for nominal income and prices in the long run and has an important effect on fluctuations in nominal and real income in the short run. Money does not matter, however, over the long run for real magnitudes. The real wealth of a society depends on its institutional structure, abilities, initiatives, driving force of its people, investment potentialities, technology etc. How many dollars the output will be valued at is the issue for which money matters.

Friedman did not take the expected rate of return on money to be a constant, as did Keynes, and by assuming that the demand for money depends on the incentives for holding other assets relative to money, he argued that the demand for money is insensitive to interest rates. Friedman's theory suggests that although the demand for money is sensitive to changes in the incentives for holding other assets relative to money, these incentives stay relatively constant when interest rate change, implying that the demand for money is insensitive to interest rates.

---

[5] See Serletis (2001) for details.

Further, Friedman suggested that the demand for money function is highly stable, implying that the quantity of money demanded can be predicted accurately by the money demand function. His view that the demand for money is insensitive to interest rates, this means that the velocity of money is highly predictable. It is therefore said that a permanent change in income changes permanent income by the same amount, whereas a temporary change in income changes permanent income by a small amount. Friedman's theory of demand for money is a reformulation of the quantity theory of money, because it leads to the quantity theory conclusion that money is the primary determinant of aggregate nominal spending.

2.2.3. Other Money Demand Models

Other transactions theories of money demand are the Baumol-Tobin model, the Shopping-Time model and Cash-in-Advance models.[6] Baumol (1952) and Tobin (1956) analyse the costs and benefits of holding money. The Baumol-Tobin model shows how the use of money in completely foreseen transactions implies economies of scale. Here the interest rate elasticity is expected to be significantly different from zero. It is noted that the Baumol-Tobin model does focus on the role of money as a medium of exchange in goods/services market. However, it does not pay attention to the holding of money in terms of the transactions facilitating services provided by money. Money demand models such as Shopping Time and Cash-in-Advance focuses explicitly on transactions services.

Theories of the demand for money that emphasize the role of money as a store of value are known as asset or portfolio theories. These models emphasize that people hold money as part of their portfolio of assets and predicts that demand for money depends on the return and risk offered by money and other assets that people can hold instead of money. Serletis (2001) states that portfolio models are theoretically interesting, but unrealistic since they ignore money's most obvious characteristic that is its ability to function as a medium of exchange. However, according to Laidler (1993) portfolio theories of demand for money have important implications for how the economy works.

---

[6] Serletis (2001) contains detailed analysis of Baumol-Tobin, Shopping-Time and Cash-in-Advance models.

2.3. Monetary Policy Targets and Instruments

In what follows I will shed some light on the relative importance of targeting money supply or the rate of interest by the central banks. The main instruments that central banks can use are money supply or interest rate. It is obvious that no central bank can use both instruments at the same time. Further, in many countries, central banks also manage the exchange rates. To this end, it could be said that the main objective of a central bank is to maintain the internal and external value of currency. If inflation rate is increasing, it indicates that the domestic value of the currency is declining. If there are persistent trade deficits, then it is an indication that the external value of the currency is under threat. Therefore, a central bank, with a managed system of exchange rate may let the exchange rate to vary in narrow limits. As a result exchange rate is another policy instrument that could be used to correct the balance of trade or payment problems.

The main issue is that how a central bank selects either money supply or rate of interest as its monetary policy instrument? This can be explained with the *ISLM* analysis. The following Figure-1 is where the *IS* curve shows instability. The main causes of instability in *IS* could be because of volatility in investment and/or exports. Suppose the central bank targets the rate of interest and wants to keep it at r^*, income may fluctuate from Y_A to Y_B. To maintain the rate of interest at r^*, the central bank has to adjust money supply passively. That is, increase money supply when *IS* shifts up or decrease money supply when *IS* shifts down. On the other hand, if the central bank targets money supply, it will leave *LM* where it is. The rate of interest will fluctuate. The range of variation in income is now smaller between Y_C and Y_D. Thus, when there is instability in *IS*, fluctuations in income can be reduced by targeting money supply.

Now, we examine the case when *LM* becomes unstable. It is worth noting that instability in *LM* is only due to instability in the demand for money function. Since 1980s many developed countries have liberalized their financial markets and this led to a strong growth and competition in the financial sector. Banks and non-bank financial institutions have developed close substitutes, especially for *M1* because interest rate on demand deposits used to be zero. This led to rapid and unpredictable changes to the demand for narrow and broad money. For example, the income elasticity of demand for *M1* in the developed countries used to be close to unity until financial markets were liberalized. Since then this elasticity has slowly and unpredictably changed and declined. Currently income elasticities for *M1* in the developed countries is around 0.5. In a sense, one can perhaps use this as an indicator of the progress in the financial sector of a country. The more is the income elasticity the more backward is that country's financial progress.

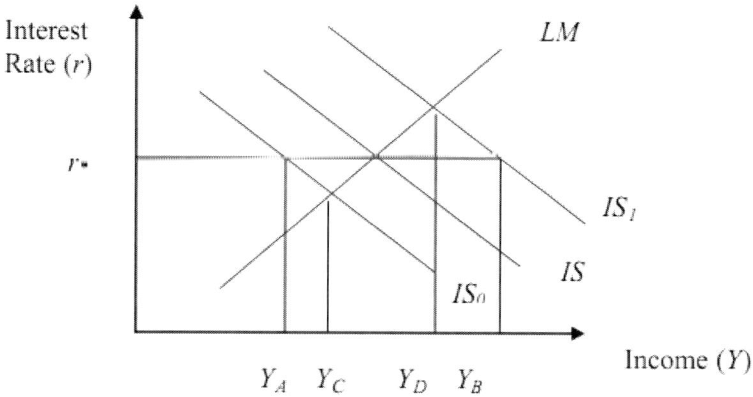

Figure 1. Instability in *IS* Curve.

The liberalization of financial markets has caused instability in the money demand functions in the developed countries. It is clear that if *LM* is unstable, respective monetary authorities should use the rate of interest as the monetary policy instrument to minimize fluctuations in income; see Poole (1970). This illustration is given in Figure 2. In Figure 2, the instability in the demand for money has caused the *LM* to shift up and down. For convenience, we assume that *IS* is stable. The main objective in using money supply as a policy instrument is to keep equilibrium in the money market. If so, the central bank has to reduce money supply when the demand for money declines and increase money supply when demand for money increases. In that case, in Figure 2, *LM* will fluctuate between *LM1* and *LM*2 and income and interest rate fluctuate between Y_A to Y_B and r_1 to r_2. On the other hand if the central bank targets the rate of interest at r^*, it will increase money supply to maintain interest rate at the target rate of r^*. Similarly, when the demand for money falls, it will use open market operations to decrease money supply and maintain interest rate at r^*.

It is noteworthy that when the interest rate is maintained at r^*, there are no fluctuations in income as shown in Figure-2. From this analysis we can say that whether a central bank should target money supply or the rate of interest depends on whether *IS* or *LM* is more unstable. Since in many advanced countries *LM* is found to be unstable – due to financial innovations – they have abandoned their earlier policy of targeting money supply and switched to interest rate targeting. However, interest rate targeting, when *LM* is stable is not appropriate. In developing countries, there is still scope for money supply targeting and the choice between the targets depends on whether *IS* or *LM* is unstable.

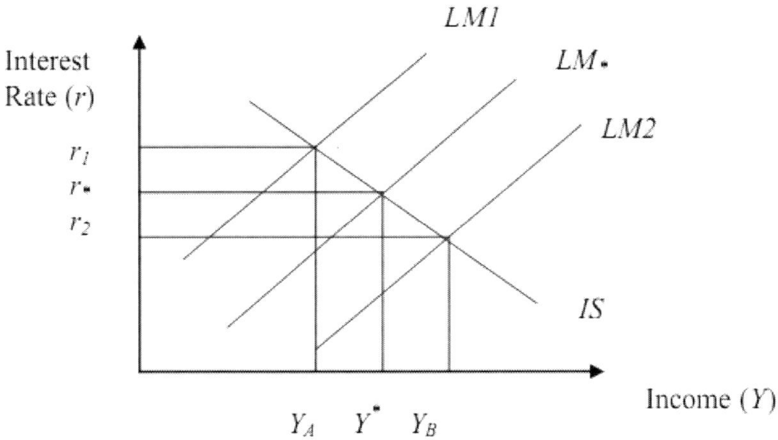

Figure 2. Instability in *LM* Curve.

Following the advanced countries, many developing countries have also switched to the rate of interest as the monetary policy instrument. Fiji has switched to interest rate targeting probably in 1997, on the basis of some empirical works showing that the demand for money has become unstable in Fiji; see Katafono (2001). However, there are some studies which show that the demand for money is stable in Fiji; see Rao and Singh (2005a), Rao and Kumar (2007a) and Singh and Kumar (2006a and 2006b). Therefore, we may say that the Reserve Bank of Fiji (RBF) may have to re-think about using the rate of interest as its monetary policy instrument.

2.4. Financial Reforms and Instability in the Money Demand

Reforms can be considered as the introduction of new products and technologies to a market or the improvement and modernization of the existing ones. In general, reforms play significant role in improvement of an economic efficiency and productivity. Consequently, under financial reforms we can consider the creation of the new financial markets, instruments, and institutions in the financial services industry. There is a natural desire of the economists throughout the world to estimate the level of the impact of financial reforms on the monetary variables, particularly, on the demand for money.

A financial system's contribution to the economy depends upon the quantity and quality of its services and the efficiency with which it provides them. Financial reforms have been the major priority since 1980's in developing and developed countries. Many researchers have argued that financial reforms have made the demand for money functions unstable in both developed and developing countries. We argue that such conclusions are only viable if appropriate demand for money stability tests shows instability and these financial reforms had significant effects. If reforms are not strong enough and weakly implemented, they may not have any significant effects or they may take a long time to be effective. The inherent efficiencies, which are expected of a financial sector, may not yet manifest in a developing country for these reasons. To some extent financial reforms have caused the instability in the demand for money functions in the advanced countries but in developing countries it needs to be examined carefully.

In his classic paper of Poole (1970) he discusses the optimal choice of monetary policy instruments within a standard *ISLM* model. He assumed that the monetary authority can control one of the two instruments of monetary policy exactly ie, money supply or interest rate. If the aim is to minimize the squared deviation of real output from its target value, Poole showed that the choice of the optimal instrument depends on the variance of the error term in the *LM* function, the covariance of the two error terms, and the size of the parameters. Further, it is interesting to know that if the use of the interest rate as a monetary policy instrument by the developing countries can be justified on the basis of the Poole's analysis.

Following financial reforms, the money demand functions may have become unstable in advanced countries. Advanced countries offer the opportunity for more and diversified financial instruments by their central banks and there are more opportunities for increased savings, improved efficiency with which resources are allocated among alternative investment projects, high standard of living and thus higher rate of economic growth. There are also more non-bank financial institutions with established track record. Such diversification in the financial system of an economy ensures that capital is mobilized from several avenues than from the traditional banking sector. The underdeveloped financial markets in most developing countries generally lack these features.

As a case study let us examine Fiji. Since 1980's due to financial reforms, there has been indeed some development in Fiji's financial sector. During

1997 the RBF reviewed its monetary policy framework where interest rate was chosen as the monetary policy instrument and the channel of transmitting monetary policy changes. Prior to interest rate targeting, the main conduct of monetary policy was through money supply. The rate of interest to be an effective tool of monetary policy, it is vital to verify that fluctuations in economic activity are due to fluctuations in the *LM* relation, which in turn is due to instability in the demand for money. In RBF studies, Katafono (2001), who was a staff researcher, found that demand for money is unstable in Fiji. Perhaps this could be the justification for the RBF to switch from money supply to interest rate as the monetary policy instrument. There have been no significant changes in the number of financial institutions, competition between banks and a market oriented interest rate policy. It is hard to expect that the demand for money in Fiji has become unstable.

CONCLUSION

This Chapter emphasized the importance of studying demand for money in the light of theories of demand for money, money supply targeting and financial reforms and the conduct of monetary policy. The main objective of estimating demand for money equations is that it has implications for monetary policy. With this perspective, we shall review some empirical works in the following chapter.

Chapter 3

EMPIRICAL LITERATURE

3.1. INTRODUCTION

In this chapter, I review several empirical studies on the demand for money in the industrial and developing countries. There is a vast amount of literature on demand for money and the majority of the studies is on the advanced industrial countries. More recently there is also a growing number of studies analyzing demand for money in the developing countries, primarily triggered by the tendency of moving towards flexible exchange rate regimes, globalization of capital markets and financial liberalization.

Tables 1 and 2 summarizes the long run income elasticities and the semi-elasticities or elasticities of opportunity cost and other variables from industrial and developing countries.[1] We have not reported the short run dynamics because they can be potentially complicated and therefore the tables concentrates only on the long run results. In order to promote comparability, the results are shown only for those studies which reported the long run cointegrating relationship of demand for money. In most cases where more than one cointegration relationship is found, results are reported only for the preferred cointegration vector(s) as identified by the author(s) which economically make sense with correct signs and magnitudes of the variables.

The purpose of this chapter is to study the long run elasticities of demand for money from existing studies. More importantly, we are interested to know what these studies have provided for stability of demand for money functions in the industrial and developing countries. This chapter is organized as follows: Sections 2 and 3 briefly discusses the money demand empirical works

[1] In Tables 1 and 2 $\ln Y$ is the logarithm of real income, R is the nominal rate of interest, $\ln E$ is the logarithm of real effective exchange rate and P is the rate of inflation.

on industrial and developing countries, respectively. Finally conclusions are in Section 4.

3.2. INCOME ELASTICITY OF MONEY DEMAND IN INDUSTRIAL COUNTRIES

The existence of a vast amount of empirical studies on demand for money on industrial countries is because consistent data series are available from the IMF and the World Bank databases. However, I only review some recent empirical works for Australia, Austria, Canada, Denmark, France, Germany, Greece, Italy, Japan, Netherlands, New Zealand, Switzerland, United Kingdom and United States. The long run elasticities of demand for money of these industrial countries are presented in Table 1.[2]

De Brouwer et al., (1993) employed quarterly data from 1970(Q3) to 1991(Q10) to estimate demand for money *M0, M1, M2* and *M3* for Australia.[3] The time series methods of the Engle Granger (EG) and Johansen (JML) were applied to estimate the cointegrating equations. The results for *M1* was not reported because the cointegrating vector of *M1* was not meaningful, that is, the coefficients of income and the two-year bond yield were signed inconsistently with theory. The EG results were not reported for demand for broad money (*M2*). However, the JML procedure provided income elasticity of *M2* around 1.3. Further, the null of no cointegration between *M3*, real income and interest rates was rejected by the JML procedure.

Felmingham and Zhang (2001) estimated demand for broad money (*M2*) for Australia using JML technique. The Gregory and Hansen approach was also used to test for structural breaks in the cointegrating relationship. They used monthly data from 1976(M3) to 1998(M4). The JML based long run income elasticity of money demand (*M2*) is 1.2. Their Gregory and Hansen tests reveals that cointegration still applies to broad money demand when there is a substantial break occurring in the last quarter of 1991. This break occurs in the midst of a deep recession and follows substantial revisions of both fiscal and monetary policy. Thus they found that the demand for money (*M2*) is stable over the period 1976 to 1998 subject to a regime shift occurring during

---

[2] Absolute *t*-ratios are reported in the parentheses. * and ** denotes significance at 5% and 10% levels, respectively.

[3] Studies on demand for money in Australia are Swamy (1987), De Brouwer et.al (1993), Lim (1995), Asano (1999), Felmingham and Zhang (2001), Mark and Sul (2003), Valadkhani (2005).

the 1991 recession in Australia. This supports the findings by Asano (1999) that demand for money is stable in Australia.

Mark and Sul (2003) used panel Dynamic Ordinary Least Squares (DOLS) to estimate coefficients of the long run money demand (*M1*) function from a panel of 19 countries with annual observations that span from 1957 to 1996.[4] They assumed that the demand for money depends on real GDP and nominal short term interest rate. Combining observations across countries allowed them to obtain long run estimates for large number of developed countries. For Australia, the income elasticity with trend is about 0.07. The stability tests were not conducted in their study.

The recent studies on demand for money in Austria are Hayo (2000) and Mark and Sul (2003).[5] Hayo (2000) used quarterly data from 1965(Q1) to 1996(Q3) to estimate the demand for real money *M1*, *M2*, and *M3* for Austria. The modelling takes place within the JML framework. The money demand was specified in the standard way, with a scale variable (GDP) and interest rate to capture the opportunity costs of holding money. The income elasticity was constraint to unity in all the cases. The interest rate coefficients have expected signs and magnitudes. Thus, they found that a stable money demand exists for all monetary aggregates in Austria. The Mark and Sul (2003) estimate of income elasticity with trend for Austria is high as 1.55 but without trend is 0.9.

Haug and Lucas (1996) used DOLS to estimate demand for *M1* for Canada using quarterly data from 1953(Q1) to 1990(Q4). They obtained an income elasticity around 0.4. This is consistent with Georgopoulos (2000). Georgopoulos (2000) employed quarterly data from 1953(Q4) to 1991(Q3) and found income elasticity for *M1* around 0.4 for Canada. In addition, Georgopoulos found a stable demand for money relationship in Canada from 1953 to 1991. Other studies on demand for money in Canada are White (1979), Ebrill (1989), McPhail (1991), Lucas and Haug (1992), Shekar and Hafizur (1996), Haug (1999 and 2006). On the stability of money demand, McPhail (1991) and Haug (1999) obtained an unstable demand for *M2* in Canada. There are only a few empirical studies on money demand for Denmark. The most recent is Mark and Sul (2003) in which the income elasticity is 0.68. The interest rate elasticity has also expected sign and

[4] These countries are Austria, Belgium, Denmark, Finland, France, Germany, Iceland, Ireland, Netherlands, Norway, Portugal, Spain, Switzerland, UK, Japan, Australia, New Zealand, Canada and USA.

[5] The earlier studies are Ziegelschmidt (1985) and Komlos (1987).

magnitude. Other studies on Denmark are Cassard et al., (1997), Juselius (1998) and La Cour (1992 and 1999).[6]

Yildirim (2003) estimated the demand for broad money (*M2*) with JML technique and quarterly data from 1978(Q3) to 1993(Q4) for France, UK, Netherlands, Germany and Italy. The long run estimates in all cases have expected signs. The income elasticity of demand for broad money for Germany is 2.2. Except Germany, the income elasticity for France, UK, Netherlands and Italy are constraint to unity.[7] Their major findings about currency substitution reveal that an increased degree of currency substitution in the EU countries could bring instability in the national money demand functions while an EU-wide money demand function could be more stable. The Mark and Sul (2003) estimate of income elasticity for France is 0.8. Other studies on money demand in France are Ram (1982), Dooley and Spinelli (1989) and Cassard et. al (1997). Cassard et al., (1997) presents evidence supporting the existence of a stable money demand relationship for France plus a core group of countries—Belgium, Denmark, Germany, Luxembourg and the Netherlands.

Bundesbank (1995) using the EG procedure obtained an income elasticity of 1.4, implausibly high for Germany. Similarly Mark and Sul (2003) obtained implausible income elasticity of around 2.2 for Germany. A more influential work for Germany is Lutkepohl and Wolters (1998). Lutkepohl and Wolters (1998) used quarterly data from 1976(Q1) to 1996(Q4) to construct a small macroeconomic model for Germany, starting from a German money demand relation for *M3*. They estimated the money demand cointegrating relation using the simple Stock (1987) approach. Note that the income elasticity is constraint to unity. Moreover, the *CUSUM* and *CUSUM SQUARES* stability tests showed that there exists a stable demand for money (*M3*) in Germany. Other studies on demand for money in Germany are Akhtar and Putnam (1980), Herz and Roeger (1990), Bruggemann and Nautz (1997), Lutkepohl et al., (1998), Hamori and Hamori (1999), Arnold (2003) and Herwatz and Reimers (2003).[8]

---

[6] The stability tests by Cassard et.al (1997) showed that demand for money is stable overtime in Denmark.

[7] For detailed analysis of demand for money in Italy, see Angelini et.al (1993), Nielson et.al (2004) and Caruso (2006). Nielson et.al (2004) estimated demand for *M2* for Italy for the period 1972 to 1998 within an error correction framework. The currency substitution between Italy and Germany is incorporated into the model. By accounting for structural breaks and currency substitution a stable money demand function is found in Italy.

[8] Hamori and Hamori (1999) found a stable relationship between money supply and real economic activity, and the money demand function was stable prior to German re-

The empirical works on money demand for Greece are Papadopoulos and Zis (1997), Ericsson and Sharma (1998), Karfakis and Opoulos (2000), Loizos and Thompson (2001) and Bahmani-Oskooee and Economidou (2005). Loizos and Thompson (2001) employed quarterly data from 1963(Q2) to 1998(Q3) and estimated demand for narrow money (*M1*) for Greece using the JML technique. They used real industrial production as a proxy for real income. The income elasticity is about 0.8. The elasticity with respect to interest rate and inflation rate have expected signs and are plausible. Bahmani-Oskooee and Economidou (2005) used quarterly data from 1975(Q1) to 2002(Q4) to estimate demand for *M1* and *M2* for Greece with the JML procedure. In formulating the money demand function, they assumed that the demand for money depends on a measure of income and rate of interest. Bahmani-Oskooee and Economidou used different interest rates in order to search for a long run relationship. Using the treasury bill rate, the income elasticity is 0.75 and semi-interest rate elasticity is -0.003. Further, their income elasticity for *M2* is high (around 1.4) and the interest rate elasticity shows a positive sign. Using the *CUSUM* and *CUSUM SQUARES* stability tests they found that the demand for narrow money is stable in Greece. However, the broad money demand did not showed a stable relationship. Other empirical works such as Papadopoulos and Zis (1997), Ericsson and Sharma (1998), Karfakis and Opoulos (2000) also tested for the stability of money demand function in Greece.[9]

---

unification. The stability of money demand tends to be rejected, however, when the sample period is extended to cover German re-unification. Lutkepohl et.al (1998) using seasonally unadjusted quarterly data from 1961(Q1) to 1990(Q2) found that the money demand (*M1*) equation is both linear and stable. After extending the sampling period until 1995(Q4) a clear structural instability due to the monetary unification on 1 July 1990 is found. Arnold (2003) found that a cointegrating relationship between real per capita deposits, real per capita income and the short-term interest rate is found in the Western states, suggesting that re-unification has not destabilized monetary relationships within West-Germany. Herwatz and Reimers (2003) using quarterly data from 1975(Q1) to 1995(Q4) which contains the German unification period showed that demand for money is stable in Germany.

[9] Papadopoulos and Zis (1997) investigated the determinants and the stability of the demand for money in Greece. The findings of their work suggest that the demand for *M1* is unstable in Greece. Ericsson and Sharma (1998) developed a constant, data-coherent, equilibrium correction model for broad money demand (*M3*) in Greece over 1976 to 1994. In spite of financial innovation, financial liberalization, and large fluctuations in the inflation rate, their estimated *M3* model is remarkably stable in Greece. Karfakis and Opoulos (2000) examined the existence and the stability of the long run demand for narrow money balances (*M1*) in Greece over the deregulated period 1986(Q1) to 1995(Q4). An interesting aspect of the stability analysis is the evidence that the long run money demand equation is stable over the sample period, implying that the narrow money aggregate could have been used as an intermediate target of monetary policy in Greece.

Maki and Kitasaka (2006) investigated the long run relationship of real narrow money (*M1*) for Japan by using threshold cointegration tests, which allows for asymmetric adjustment, introduced by Enders and Siklos (2001). The threshold cointegration approach provides clear evidence of the cointegration relationship between money, income, interest rate and prices in Japan. They found that the demand for money is stable in Japan only if unit income elasticity is imposed. This finding is similar to Lucas (1988) for USA. Other previous studies on money demand for Japan are Hoffman and Rasche (1991), Arize and Shwiff (1993), Fujiki and Mulligan (1996), Fujiki (1999), Amano and Wirjanto (2000), Bahmani-Oskooee (2001), Nagayasu (2003) and Miyagawa and Morita (2004).[10]

There exists only a few studies on money demand for Netherlands. For instance see, Traa (1991), Fase and Winder (1990 and 1996), Yildirim (2003) and Mark and Sul (2003).[11] The Mark and Sul estimate of income elasticity with trend is 0.3 and is generally plausible for Netherlands. For New Zealand, Orden and Fisher (1993) employed quarterly data from 1965(Q2) to 1989(Q4) to estimate demand for *M3* with JML technique. The implied income elasticity is around 0.4. Valadkhani (2003) examined the long run determinants of the demand for *M3* in New Zealand by employing the JML technique and quarterly data for the period 1988(Q1) to 2002(Q2). He finds that the demand for money is cointegrated with real income, the spread between interest on money and on non-money assets, the expected rate of inflation and the real effective exchange rate. Choi and Oxley (2004) also supports Valadkhani (2003) that there exists a long run relationship of demand for money in New Zealand.

Chowdhury (1995) used quarterly data from 1973(Q2) to 1991(Q4) to estimate demand for *M1* for Switzerland with JML technique. The income elasticity is around 0.9. In a recent study, Gerlach-Kristen (2001) used annual data from 1936 to 1995 to estimate demand for *M3* for Switzerland. They utilized the JML procedure to investigate the long run relationship of money demand. The income elasticity is high as 1.259. The interest rate spread has a coefficient of -0.221 with correct sign and magnitude.

---

[10] Bahmani-Oskooee (2001) employed the ARDL approach combined with *CUSUM* and *CUSUM SQUARES* tests to show that not only *M2* is cointegrated with income and interest rate, but the estimated relation is stable in Japan. Fujiki and Mulligan (1996), Amano and Wirjanto (2000) and Miyagawa and Morita (2004) also found that demand for money relation is stable overtime in Japan. Nagayasu (2003) also studied the stability of the Japanese money demand function but concludes that the money demand function is unstable.

[11] We did not get access to Fase and Winder studies for review.

More importantly, they obtained a stable demand for money function for Switzerland. Other studies on money demand for Switzerland are Krishnakumar and Gueye (1998), Peytrignet and Stahel (1998) and Baltensperger et al., (2001). An important finding by Peytrignet and Stahel (1998) is that Switzerland's *M2* and *M3* aggregates are stable overtime.

Hendry and Ericsson (1991) employed quarterly data from 1963(Q1) to 1989(Q2) to develop a parsimonious conditional equilibrium correction model for demand for money (*M1*) for U.K. Hendry and Ericsson assumed that real narrow money depends on real total final expenditure and net interest rate (R_t^{net}).[12] It is worth noting that the income elasticity is constraint to unity.[13] The semi-elasticity with respect to net interest rate is around -0.6. Drake and Chrystal (1994) and Mark and Sul (2003) obtained high income elasticity for the U.K. Other studies on money demand for U.K are Drake (1996), Nielsen (2004), Escribano (2004) and Caporale and Gil-Alana (2005). While Nielsen (2004) and Escribano (2004) argues that the long run structures of money demand are reasonably stable in U.K, Caporale and Gil-Alana (2005) to some extent found instability in the U.K money demand and therefore opposes monetary targeting by the central bank.

Baba, Hendry and Starr (1992) using quarterly data from 1960(Q3) to 1988(Q3) estimated demand for *M1* for USA with the JML technique. The income elasticity is plausible (around 0.5). This is comparable to Ball (1998) with similar income elasticity for USA. Further McNown and Wallace (1992) and Mark and Sul (2003) estimate of income elasticity for USA is around unity. Yossifov (1998) found an income elasticity that is negatively signed, perhaps explaining some structural change features in the economy. Other studies such as Hafer and Jansen (1991) and Miyao (1996) found that there exists a long run relationship of demand for money in the USA.[14] Earlier studies such as Gibson (1972) and Serletis (1987) on USA are more methodological based.

---

[12] The R_t^{net} is calculated as $R^{LA} - R^{SDa}$. R^{LA} is the three month local authority interest rate and R^{SDa} is the retail sight-deposit interest rate. The interest rates are measured in percent per annum, expressed as fractions. The first interest rate is the dominant short-term interest rate in the secondary market and measures the return on assets outside *M1*. The latter interest rate is on checkable interest-bearing accounts at commercial banks and is a return on an asset within *M1*.

[13] A similar approach was also taken by Yildirim (2003).

[14] We did not get access to these studies for further review.

3.3. Income Elasticity of Money Demand in Developing Countries

The demand for money on developing countries have received enormous attention in the recent years. In this book, I only review some recent empirical works for Bangladesh, Cameroon, Chile, Egypt, Fiji, Gambia, India, Indonesia, Iran, Israel, Ivory Coast, Jamaica, Kenya, Malaysia, Mauritania, Mexico, Morocco, Niger, Nigeria, Pakistan, Papua New Guinea, Philippines, Sierra Leone, Singapore, Somalia, South Africa and Thailand. The long run elasticities of demand for money of these developing countries are presented in Table 2.[15]

Bangladesh has quite a few empirical works on money demand. Siddiki (2000) used annual data from 1975 to 1995 to estimate the demand for broad money (*M2*) for Bangladesh with the bounds test (ARDL) approach. Siddiki's estimate of income elasticity at 3.26 seems a bit high. The implied interest rate elasticity has the expected negative sign and its magnitude is plausible. But the coefficient of the proxy for the effects of the foreign interest rate is insignificant at the conventional levels. Valadkhani and Alauddin (2003) have obtained low income elasticity around 0.3 for Bangladesh.[16] Hossain (2006) estimated the demand for narrow and broad money for Bangladesh using the somewhat outdated partial adjustment mechanism (*PAM*).[17] The income elasticity of demand for *M1* is significant and around unity. The interest rate elasticity has correct negative sign but is insignificant even at the 10 % level. Further, his *CUSUM SQUARES* stability tests indicate that demand for *M1* is unstable during the period 1973 to 2003, but when the model is estimated for the sub-sample period 1985 to 2003, it is found to be stable, indicating significant structural changes. In a more recent study, Rao and Kumar (2007b) found income elasticity of demand for *M1* in Bangladesh about 1.26. They

[15] Absolute *t*-ratios are reported in the parentheses. * and ** denotes significance at 5% and 10% levels, respectively.

[16] Valadkhani and Alauddin (2003) utilized panel cointegration technique to examine the major determinants of the demand for real money balances (*M2*) for eight developing countries viz., Malaysia, Chile, Thailand, Papua New Guinea (PNG), Bangladesh, Sri Lanka, Sierra Leone and Philippines. Pooling cross-country and time series data for the period 1979 to 1999 and employing the Seemingly Unrelated Regression (SUR) estimation technique, they modelled the standard money demand function.

[17] Another study by Hossain (1993) on the demand for money for Bangladesh used quarterly data from 1976(Q1) to 1989(Q4) and found that the income elasticity for narrow money was low at 0.63.

also obtained a stable demand for money function for Bangladesh.[18] Similar findings by Kumar (2007) on income elasticity and stability of money demand in Bangladesh.[19]

There are only two studies for Cameroon, see Fielding (1994) and Nachega (2001). Fielding (1994) used quarterly data to estimate demand for broad money (*M2*) for four African countries viz., Cameroon, Nigeria, Ivory Coast and Kenya. The JML procedure was used to test and estimate the cointegrating equations. For Cameroon, the income elasticity is around 1.5. Nachega (2001) applied error correction model to investigate the stability of demand for broad money in Cameroon from 1963 to 1993. He obtained unit income elasticity and supports monetary targeting by central bank because demand for money is found to be stable in Cameroon. Ewing and Payne (1999) estimated demand for money (*M1* and *M2*) for Chile with quarterly data from 1980(Q1) to 1996(Q1). The JML technique provided income elasticity for *M1* and *M2* around 0.8 and 1.4, respectively. They found that demand for *M1* and *M2* is stable in Chile when exchange rate is incorporated in the model. Other studies on money demand for Chile are Arrau and Gregorio (1993), Adam (2000) and Soto and Tapia (2001). The recent study by Soto and Tapia (2001) found that the estimated demand for money in Chile is remarkably stable in spite of the profound structural and financial reforms carried out throughout the 1977 to 2000 period. For Egypt, Arize et al.,'s (1990) estimate of income elasticity of *M1* is 0.4.[20] Their findings suggest that demand for money is stable in African countries.

---

[18] Rao and Kumar (2007b) have used the Gregory and Hansen technique for structural breaks to estimate the demand for real narrow money for Bangladesh for the period 1973 to 2003. Their study reveals that there exists a cointegrating relationship between real narrow money, real income and nominal rate of interest after allowing for structural breaks. However, of the four possible structural breaks, the one with an intercept shift in 1989 yields meaningful cointegrating coefficients. Their estimates imply that there is a well-determined and stable demand for money in Bangladesh from 1988 to 2003 and perhaps following the financial reforms in the 1980s, demand for narrow money has declined by a small amount. Therefore, they conclude that money supply is the appropriate monetary policy instrument to be targeted by the Central Bank of Bangladesh.

[19] Kumar (2007) estimated demand for narrow money for Bangladesh using GETS and JML techniques. He used annual data from 1973 to 2003. The JML based cointegrating vector implies that the implied income elasticity of demand for money is about unity and the interest rate elasticity at the mean rate of 9.22% is about -0.176. Similarly, the GETS approach gave an unit income elasticity and plausible interest rate elasticity. His *CUSUM* and *CUSUM SQUARES* stability tests showed that the demand for narrow money is stable and therefore monetary targeting is feasible in Bangladesh.

[20] Arize et.al (1990) used Two Stage Least Squares (TSLS) technique to estimate demand for narrow money (*M1*) for seven African countries with annual data from 1960 to 1987. The countries are Egypt, Gambia, Mauritania, Morocco, Niger, Nigeria and Somalia. The

Studies on demand for money in Fiji are limited.[21] Rao and Singh (2005a) have applied alternative time series approaches of GETS and JML with annual data for Fiji from 1971 to 2002. They found that demand for money (*M1*) in Fiji is stable and well determined. The implied income elasticity in JML is not significantly different from unity as their Wald test on the null of unit income elasticity was not rejected at the 5% level. The implied long run semi-interest rate elasticity is also plausible with correct negative sign. These observations are further justified by their GETS estimates. Later Rao and Singh (2005b) have used Hendry and Krolzig's PcGets software and arrived at the same conclusion about the income and interest rate elasticities.[22] In a more recent study, Rao and Kumar (2007a) used the Gregory and Hansen procedure to test the stability of the demand for narrow money in Fiji for the period 1970 to 2002. They found that a stable demand for *M1* persists in Fiji even in presence of structural breaks in the model.[23]

India has a handful of studies on money demand, see for example Bhattacharya (1974), Kamath (1985), Moosa (1992), Rao and Shalabh (1995), Das and Mandal (2000), Ramachandran (2004), Rao and Singh (2005c) and Bahmani-Oskooee and Rehman (2005). We only study the recent empirical works that is by Rao and Singh (2005c) and Bahmani-Oskooee and Rehman (2005). Rao and Singh (2005c) estimated the demand for money (*M1*) for India with annual data from 1953 to 2003. Using the JML technique they obtained the cointegrating equation which implies that in the long run the income elasticity of demand for money is about 1.2 and the interest rate elasticity at the mean rate of 7.65% is about -0.18. Moreover, they found that the demand for money is temporally stable in India and therefore monetary

---

demand for money was assumed to be a function of real GDP, inflation rates, foreign interest rates, expected exchange rates, and capital mobility. The coefficient of capital mobility is insignificant at conventional levels in all cases. Note that their income elasticities range from 0.2 to 0.5. Thus, they claim that the demand for money is stable in all the selected African countries.

[21] These are Luckett (1987), Jayaraman and Ward (2000), Katafono (2001), Rao and Singh (2005a and 2005b), Singh and Kumar (2006a and 2006b) and Rao and Kumar (2007a). Studies prior to Rao and Singh (2005a) has limitations and these are well detailed in Rao and Singh (2005a).

[22] This automated software searches for the optimal dynamic lag structure by minimizing the path-dependency bias. In contrast, in the GETS estimation variable deletion tests are used to obtain the final parsimonious specifications and these procedures are not free from the aforesaid path-dependency bias. The dynamic structure obtained by Rao and Singh (2005b) with PcGets is not significantly from what is in Rao and Singh (2005a) but has marginally improved the summary statistics.

[23] Similar findings by Jayaraman and Ward (2000) and Singh and Kumar (2006a and 2006b) that demand for money is stable overtime in Fiji.

targeting by the Central Bank of India is feasible.[24] In another recent study, Bahmani-Oskooee and Rehman (2005) used quarterly data from 1973 to 2000 to estimate the demand for money for seven Asian countries: India, Indonesia, Malaysia, Pakistan, Philippines, Singapore and Thailand.[25] Using ARDL approach they achieved low income elasticities for India, Philippines and Thailand. Further their *CUSUM* stability tests showed that the demand for narrow money is stable in all the selected countries. However using *CUSUM SQUARES* stability tests, the money demand functions for India, Malaysia and Pakistan showed some instability.

Price and Insukindro (1994) using EG procedure found income elasticity of *M1* as 1.3 for Indonesia. Similar findings on income elasticity is attained by Bahmani-Oskooee and Rehman (2005) for Indonesia. Anglingkusumo (2005) used JML technique to estimate demand for *M1* for Indonesia for the period between 1981(Q1) to 2002(Q4). The major finding of their study is that demand for *M1* is stable in Indonesia. Other studies on money demand for Indonesia are Dekle and Pradhan (1997), McNelis (1998), James (2005) and Narayan (2007). The recent studies by James (2005) and Narayan (2007) argue that financial liberalization plays a key role in determining money demand and its fluctuations in Indonesia.

The studies on money demand for Iran are Moradi (1999), Bahmani-Oskooee (2003) and Bahmani-Oskooee and Rehman (2005). In the most recent study, Bahmani-Oskooee and Rehman (2005) obtained plausible income elasticity around 1.3 for Iran. Israel also has very few empirical works on money demand, see Yashiv (1994), Melnick (1995) and Kogar (1995). Kogar (1995) used quarterly data for Israel for the period 1977(Q1) to 1988(Q4) to estimate the demand for narrow money (*M1*) and broad money (*M2*). The implied income elasticity based on *M1* and *M2* are around 0.5 and 0.3, respectively. For Ivory Coast, Fielding (1994) achieved an income elasticity of *M2* around 1.6.

Studies on money demand for Jamaica are Ghartey (1998), Bynoe (2002) and Atkins (2005). Atkins (2005) used JML technique to estimate demand for

[24] Similar findings by Das and Mandal (2000) and Ramachandran (2004) that demand for money is stable overtime in India.

[25] They have used the index of industrial production as the scale variable and proxy for real income (GDP). They have assumed that the real demand for money (*M1*) is a function of the index of industrial production , rate of inflation, and the exchange rate. It is worth noting that there is no rate of interest, but the rate of inflation and the exchange rate are used. Inflation rate is not a bad proxy for the nominal rate of interest but inclusion of the exchange rate is hard to justify in the demand for money for developing countries because holdings of foreign exchange is not a realistic option.

broad money for Jamaica from 1962 to 2002. All the coefficients are statistically significant but the sign for rate of interest and inflation are contrary to expectations. The income elasticity of *M2* is 1.56 is significant. Using *CUSUM* and *CUSUM SQUARES* stability tests, they found that there exists stable demand for broad money in Jamaica. For Kenya, Fielding (1994) found three cointegrating vectors. Note that none of the individual vectors reflects the data generating process for money demand.[26]

Bahmani-Oskooee and Rehman (2005) obtained significant and plausible income elasticity of *M1* around 1.2 for Malaysia. However, Valadkhani and Alauddin (2003) estimate of income elasticity for Malaysia is much lower. Marashdeh (1998) used JML technique to estimate the demand for money (*M1*) for Malaysia with quarterly data from 1980(Q1) to 1994(Q10). They used Chow tests and found that demand for *M1* is stable overtime in Malaysia. Similar findings are also by Majid (2004) and Hussain and Liew (2006) that the demand for money is stable in Malaysia.[27] Thornton (1996) used error correction approach to estimate demand for *M1* and *M2* for Mexico. Their results favor *M2* as the monetary aggregate to target in Mexico. Khamis and Leone (1999) used JML technique to estimate money demand (*M1*) for Mexico with quarterly data from 1983(Q1) to 1997(Q6). They obtained a low income elasticity of around 0.45. Cuthbertson and Galindo (1999) analysed the demand for *M1* and *M3* and in particular the presence of a portfolio balance effect for Mexico over the period 1978 to 1990. The empirical evidence indicates that there is a stable money demand function even when data from the 'crisis period' of the 1980s are included. A good analysis of demand for money and monetary policy for Mexico can be found in Arrau and Gregorio (1993) and Turner and Benavides (2001).

Arize et al., (1990) and Hoffman and Tahiri (1994) are the only empirical works for money demand in Morocco. For both Morocco and Niger, Arize et

[26] Alternative specifications of money demand should have been used to derive the long run relationship of money demand in Kenya, see Adam (1992).

[27] Majid (2004) examined the money demand in Malaysia from 1974 to 2001, a period characterised by various events particularly the financial sector liberalization, changes in monetary framework and currency crises. Their results support the existence of fairly stable long run money demand function despite the various changes and developments in the economy. They argue that monetary targeting framework in Malaysia seems to be appropriate and monetary aggregate continue to be a useful longer-term indicator in the formulation of monetary policy. Similarly, Hussain and Liew (2006) used Malaysian monthly data covering 1979(M1) to 2002(M5) and found a cointegration relationship of *M1* and *M2*. *CUSUM* stability test shows that both *M1* and *M2* are stable in this sample period, in spite of the financial innovations, liberalization and the Asian financial crisis. See also Dekle and Pradhan (1997) for detailed analysis on Asian countries.

al., (1990) found somewhat lower income elasticity (around 0.3) of *M1*. Studies on money demand for Nigeria are Arize et al., (1990), Fielding (1994), Nwaobi (2001), Anoruo (2002), Akinlo (2005), Teriba (2006) and Owoye and Onafowora (2007). Anorou (2002) tested the stability of the demand for broad money (*M2*) function for Nigeria in the Structural Adjustment Program (SAP) period. He used quarterly data from 1986(Q2) to 2000(Q1) and utilized the JML technique. The index of industrial production was used as a proxy for real income. The elasticity with respect to industrial production is 5.70. The major finding was that the Nigerian *M2* money demand function is stable in the SAP period (1986 to 2000) and money supply is a viable monetary policy tool in Nigeria. Recently, Owoye and Onafowora (2007) employed JML technique with quarterly data from 1986(Q1) to 2001(Q4) to examine demand for broad money (*M2*) in Nigeria. They obtained an income elasticity of approximately 2.1. More importantly, they found through the *CUSUM* and *CUSUM SQUARES* stability tests, the demand for broad money is stable in Nigeria.

Hussain et al., (2006) estimated demand for reserve money (*M0*), narrow money (*M1*) and broad money (*M2*) for Pakistan using annual data from 1972 to 2005. Using the JML technique the implied income elasticity with respect to *M0, M1* and *M2* are 0.75, 0.74 and 0.80, respectively. The income elasticities are comparable with Bahmani-Oskooee and Rehman (2005). However, in Hussain et al., (2006) the sign of financial innovation is negative which is contrary to expectations. The financial innovation sensitivity of money demand may indicate better management of monetary policy and therefore a positive sign is expected. Other studies on money demand for Pakistan emphasized the use of inflation rate, see for example Price and Nasim (1999) and Qayyum (2005).

The recent works on Papua New Guinea (PNG) are Arize et al., (1990) and Kannapiran (2001). Arize et al., (1990) obtained an income elasticity of around 0.6. Kannapiran (2001) applied the EG procedure to estimate demand for broad money for the period of 1979 to 1995. The income elasticity is around 0.20. For Singapore, Bahmani-Oskooee and Rehman (2005) obtained income elasticity of *M1* around 0.7. Detailed analysis of money demand and monetary policy in Asian countries can be found in Khalid (1999) and Chaisrisawatsuk et al., (2004).

Studies on money demand for South Africa are Nell (1999 and 2003), Wesso (2002) and Tlelima and Turner (2004). Nell (1999) used JML technique to investigate the long run demand for money function over the period 1965 to 1997.

Their empirical results suggest that there exists a stable long run demand for *M3* in South Africa, while the demand for *M1* and *M2* display parameter instability following financial reforms since 1980s. Wesso (2002) used JML technique to estimate demand for money (*M3*) for South Africa using quarterly data from 1971(Q1) to 2000(Q4).[28] Note that the long run income elasticity is high as 1.84.

Wesso found that the demand for money (*M3*) is structurally unstable in South Africa. Dekle and Pradhan (1997) used JML to estimate demand for *M1* for Thailand for the period 1978 to 1995. They obtained an income elasticity around 1.1. The income elasticities obtained by Valadkhani and Alauddin (2003) and Bahmani-Oskooee and Rehman (2005) are lower than unity for Thailand. In a more recent study, Sumner (2008) used ARDL procedure with annual data from 1967 to 2002 and found that the demand for money is stable overtime in Thailand.

CONCLUSIONS

In this chapter, I have surveyed empirical works that analyzed demand for money on industrial and developing countries. This study has summarized the major features of previous studies on demand for money, particularly, the long run elasticities and stability of the demand for money. The latter is very important because it has implications for the conduct of monetary policy in the country. The information presented in this survey would allow researchers to compare their own results and methods with what were undertaken previously in a wide range of countries. In this era with inflationary pressures and financial reforms, this study will help identify important factors to be considered prior estimating demand for money for other countries. In general, we noted that most of the empirical studies on money demand seems to have limitations, that is, the income elasticity of money demand is either over-estimated or under-estimated. As a result, the stability tests are also not reliable. One possible reason for this could be the limitations in data.

[28] After using 1971(Q1) to 2000(Q4) as the estimation sub-sample, a forecast was generated from 2001(Q1) to 2002(Q2) using a varying parameter regression model, which was then compared to that of the simpler money demand function. Allowing some coefficients to vary overtime also improved the forecasting performance of the money demand equation significantly over the forecasting period.

Table 1. Long run Elasticities of Demand for Money in Industrial Countries

Country/Study	Money	Period	Method	ln$Y$	R	ln$E$	P	Remarks
Australia								
De Brouwer et al., (1993)	*M2*	1970(Q3)-1991(Q10)	JML	1.352 (32.16)*	-0.004 (1.18)			For De Brouwer et al., R is treasury bill rate. They also used 2 and 10 years bond rates. The income elasticity remains around 1.35 and interest rate elasticity with very minor changes. The income elasticities for *M3* is around 2 and 3.
Felmingham and Zhang (2000)	*M2*	1976(M3)-1998(M4)	JML	1.210	0.250		-0.280	Felmingham and Zhang used interest rate spread for R.
Mark and Sul (2003)	*M1*	1957-1999	DOLS	0.068	-0.048			Mark and Sul's estimates with trend is reported. Without trend the income elasticity is 0.9 and interest rate elasticity remains same.
Austria								
Hayo (2000)	*M1*	1965(Q1)-1996(Q3)	JML	1.000				Hayo also used a step dummy variable from second quarter of 1979 to capture appreciation of schilling. This estimate is -0.23.
	M2	1965(Q1)-1996(Q3)	JML	1.000	-0.260			
	M3	1965(Q1)-1996(Q3)	JML	1.000	-0.340			
Mark and Sul (2003)	*M1*	1957-1999	DOLS	1.552	-0.037			Mark and Sul's estimates with trend is reported. Without trend the income elasticity is 0.9 and interest rate elasticity is -0.009.

Table 1. (Continued)

Country/Study	Money	Period	Method	ln*Y*	*R*	ln*E*	*P*	Remarks
Canada								
Haug and Lucas (1996)	*M1*	1953(Q1)-1990(Q4)	DOLS	0.420	-0.033			
Georgopoulos (2000)	*M1*	1953(Q4)-1991(Q3)	JML	0.431	-0.225			
Denmark								
Mark and Sul (2003)	*M1*	1957-1999	DOLS	0.684	-0.036			Only estimates with trend is reported. Without trend the income elasticity is 1.46 and interest rate elasticity is -0.043.
France								
Yildirim (2003)	*M2*	1978(Q3)-1993(Q4)	JML	1.000	-0.008		-0.670	
Mark and Sul (2003)	*M1*	1957-1999	DOLS	0.842	0.004			Mark and Sul's estimates with trend is reported. Without trend the income elasticity is 0.68 and interest rate elasticity is 0.01.
Germany								For Lutkepohl and Wolters *R* is spread between long term interest rate and own rate of *M3*.
Bundesbank (1995)	*M3*	1970(Q1)-1994(Q4)	EG	1.400	-1.220			
Lutkepohl and Wolters (1997)	*M3*	1976(Q1)-1996(Q4)	Stock	1.000	-0.582			Yildirim also used unification dummy variable (unification caused sharp jumps in population). The dummy estimate is -0.28.
Yildirim (2003)	*M2*	1979(Q1)-1993(Q4)	JML	2.210	-0.035		-0.035	
Mark and Sul (2003)	*M1*	1957-1999	DOLS	1.691	-0.023			Mark and Sul's estimates with trend is reported. Without trend the income elasticity is 0.68 and interest rate elasticity is 0.01.

Country/Study	Money	Period	Method	ln$Y$	R	ln$E$	P	Remarks
Greece								
Loizos and Thompson (2002)	*M1*	1963(Q2)-1998(Q3)	JML	0.814	-0.272		-0.189	Loizos and Thompson used real industrial production to proxy real income.
Bahmani-Oskooee and Economidou (2005)	*M1*	1975(Q1)-2002(Q4)	JML	0.750 (10.49)*	-0.003 (0.77)			Bahmani-Oskooee and Economidou used treasury bill rate for R.
	M2	1975(Q1)-2002(Q4)	JML	1.450 (3.82)*	0.113 (4.25)*			
Italy								
Yildirim (2003)	*M2*	1980(Q1)-1993(Q4)	JML	1.000	-0.002		-3.130	
Japan								
Maki and Kitasaka (2006)	*M1*	1964(M1)-2003(M4)	Enders and Siklos (2001)	0.836 (80.61)*	-0.128 (55.52)*			Enders and Siklos (2001) proposed TAR (threshold autoregression) tests.
Netherlands								
Yildirim (2003)	*M2*	1978(Q3)-1993(Q4)	JML	1.000			-0.770	Yildirim also used unification dummy variable (unification caused sharp jumps in population). The dummy estimate is -0.019.
Mark and Sul (2003)	*M1*	1957-1999	DOLS	0.309	-0.011			Mark and Sul's estimates with trend is reported. Without trend the income elasticity is 1.112 and interest rate elasticity is -0.045.

Table 1. (Continued)

Country/Study	Money	Period	Method	ln*Y*	*R*	ln*E*	*P*	Remarks
New Zealand								
Orden and Fisher (1993)	*M3*	1965(Q2)-1989(Q4)	JML	0.410	-0.014		1.130	Price level is used for *P*.
Switzerland								
Chowdhury (1995)	*M1*	1973(Q2)-1991(Q4)	JML	0.887				Chowdhury's estimate of alternative return is -0.310.
Gerlach-Kristen (2001)	*M3*	1936-1995	JML	1.259	-0.221			Gerlach-Kristen used Swiss interest rate spread (bond yield and deposit rate) for *R*.
United Kingdom								
Hendry and Ericsson (1991)	*M1*	1964(Q3)-1989(Q2)	ECM	1.000	-0.630			Hendry and Ericsson used net interest rate for *R*.
Drake and Chrystal (1994)	*M1*	1976(Q2)-1993(Q3)	JML	3.372			-3.765	Drake and Chrystal income elasticity for *M2* and *M3* is around 2.6.
Yildirim (2003)	*M2*	1978(Q3)-1993(Q4)	JML	1.000	-0.013		-0.310	Mark and Sul's estimates with trend is reported. Without trend the income elasticity is 1.738 and interest rate elasticity is -0.089.
Mark and Sul (2003)	*M1*	1957-1999	DOLS	2.128	-0.089			

Country/Study	Money	Period	Method	ln*Y*	*R*	ln*E*	*P*	Remarks
United States								
Baba, Hendry and Starr (1992)	*M1*	1960(Q3)-1988(Q3)	JML	0.510	-6.640		-5.510	Baba, Hendry and Starr also used financial innovation and volatility measure of long term bond. The estimates, respectively, are -3.960 and 3.720.
McNown and Wallace (1992)	*M1*	1973(Q2)-1988(Q4)	JML	1.001	-9.600			
	M2	1973(Q2)-1988(Q4)	JML	1.128		0.131		
Yossifov (1998)	*M2*	1972(M1)-1991(M12)	JML	-0.698	-1.747			Yossifov used real personal income for *Y*, 3 months treasury bill rate for *R*, and the estimate for own rate of return for *M2* is -0.305.
					0.220			
Mark and Sul (2003)	*M1*	1957-1999	DOLS	1.022				Mark and Sul's estimates with trend is reported. Without trend the income elasticity is 0.428 and interest rate elasticity is -0.035.
					-0.039			

Table 2. Long run Elasticities of Demand for Money in Developing Countries

Country/Study	Money	Period	Method	ln*Y*	*R*	ln*E*	*P*	Remarks
Bangladesh								
Siddiki (2000)	*M2*	1975-1995	ARDL	3.260 (10.86)*	0.088 (4.50)*			Siddiki's foreign interest rate estimate is -0.145.
Valadkhani and Alauddin (2003)	*M2*	1979-1999	SUR	0.341				
Hossain (2006)	*M1*	1973-2003	PAM	1.030 (5.73)*	-0.120 (1.41)			In PAM, Hossain's one period lagged real money estimate is 0.10.
Rao and Kumar (2007b)	*M1*	1973-2003	Gregory Hansen	1.261 (7.23)*	-0.030 (1.88)**			
Kumar (2007)	*M1*	1971-2002	JML	1.072 (12.68)*	-0.019 (2.45)*			
			GETS	1.000 (12.75)*	-0.043 (2.92)*			
Cameroon								
Fielding (1994)	*M2*	1976(Q1)-1987(Q2)	JML	1.490	-8.910		-1.310	The estimate of annual moving average is -8.1.
Chile								
Ewing and Payne (1999)	*M1*	1980(Q1)-1996(Q1)	JML	0.841 (5.07)*	-0.086 (1.39)	0.078 (0.86)		
	M2	1980(Q1)-1996(Q1)	JML	1.407 (11.35)*	-0.156 (2.24)*	-0.292 (3.84)*		

Country/Study	Money	Period	Method	ln*Y*	*R*	ln*E*	*P*	Remarks
Egypt								
Arize et .al (1990)	*M1*	1960-1987	TSLS	0.440 (2.27)*			0.850 (1.12)	The estimate of capital mobility is -0.14.
Fiji								
Rao and Singh (2005a)	*M1*	1971-2002	JML GETS	1.133 1.074 (4.22)*	-0.037 -0.036 (2.97)*			
Gambia								
Arize et al., (1990)	*M1*	1960-1987	TSLS	0.330 (1.74)**			-0.430 (0.53)	The estimate of capital mobility is -0.001.
India								
Bahmani-Oskooee and Rehman (2005)	*M1*	1973(Q1)-2000(Q4)	ARDL	0.550 (8.40)*		0.270 (5.39)*	-2.730 (3.12)*	Bahmani-Oskooee and Rehman's income elasticity for *M2* is -3.83
Rao and Singh (2005c)	*M1*	1953-2002	JML	1.190 (27.93)*	-0.023 (3.33)*			
Indonesia								
Price and Insukindro (1994)	*M1*	1969(Q1)-1987(Q4)	EG	1.300	-1.900			
Bahmani-Oskooee and Rehman (2005)	*M1*	1973(Q1)-2000(Q4)	ARDL	1.290 (2.29)*		0.650 (8.88)*	-16.690 (3.41)*	Bahmani-Oskooee and Rehman's income elasticity for *M2* is 3.92.
Iran								
Bahmani-Oskooee (1996)	*M2*	1959-1990	JML	1.330		0.020	-1.610	

Table 2. (Continued)

Country/Study	Money	Period	Method	ln*Y*	*R*	ln*E*	*P*	Remarks
Israel								
Kogar (1995)	*M1*	1977(Q1)-1988(Q4)	JML	0.481		-0.049	-0.715	
	M2	1977(Q1)-1988(Q4)	JML	0.348		-0.029	0.348	
Ivory Coast								
Fielding (1994)	*M2*	1974(Q3)-1987(Q4)	JML	1.580	-3.040		2.430	The estimate of annual moving average estimate is -1.63.
Jamaica								
Atkins (2005)	*M2*	1962-2000	JML	1.560 (13.35)*	1.460 (5.23)*		0.720 (18.04)*	*P* is the logarithm of consumer price index.
Kenya								
Fielding (1994)	*M2*	1975(Q2)-1989(Q2)	JML					The annual moving average estimate, respectively, for vectors 1, 2 and 3 are 16.627, 9.752 and 4.663. Note that Kenya has three cointegrating vectors.
			Vector-1		-0.271		0.752	
			Vector-2		-1.268		3.259	
			Vector-3		-0.528		0.861	
Malaysia								
Valadkhani and Alauddin (2003)	*M2*	1979-1999	SUR	0.567				
Bahmani-Oskooee and Rehman (2005)	*M1*	1973(Q1)-2000(Q4)	ARDL	1.200 (16.50)*		-0.640 (1.79)**	13.060 (2.13)*	Bahmani-Oskooee and Rehman's income elasticity for M2 is 1.25.

Country/Study	Money	Period	Method	ln$Y$	R	ln$E$	P	Remarks
Mauritania								
Arize et al., (1990)	*M1*	1960-1987	TSLS	0.420 (3.38)*		-0.010 (1.89)**	2.060 (20.60)*	The foreign interest rate estimate is -0.001.
Mexico								
Khamis and Leone (1999)	*M1*	1983(Q1)-1997(Q6)	JML	0.450				Alternative return estimate is -9.730. It includes both net effective exchange rate and foreign interest rates.
Morocco								
Arize et al., (1990)	*M1*	1960-1987	TSLS	0.300 (2.01)*		0.0004 (0.43)	0.440 (0.59)	The foreign interest rate estimate is -0.019.
Niger								
Arize et al., (1990)	*M1*	1960-1987	TSLS	0.320 (1.61)		-0.004 (1.55)	-0.190 (0.34)	The foreign interest rate estimate is -0.04.
Nigeria								
Fielding (1994)	*M2*	1976(Q1)-1989(Q2)	JML	0.720	1.180		-1.420	Fielding's annual moving average estimate is -4.43.
Arize et al., (1990)	*M1*	1960-1987	TSLS	0.200 (3.11)*			0.090 (0.15)	Arize et al.,'s capital mobility estimate is -0.001.
Anoruo (2002)	*M1*	1986(Q2)-2000(Q1)	JML	5.700 (8.56)*	-5.440 (7.92)*			Anoruo used real discount rate for *R*.
Owoye and Onafowora (2007)	*M2*	1986(Q1)-2001(Q4)	JML	2.067 (5.35)*	0.306 (8.19)*	-0.371 (3.91)*	-0.041 (5.05)*	Owoye and Onafowora's foreign interest rate estimate is -0.207.

Table 2. (Continued)

Country/Study	*Money*	Period	Method	lnY	R	lnE	P	Remarks
Pakistan								
Bahmani-Oskooee and Rehman (2005)	*M1*	1973(Q1)-2000(Q4)	ARDL	0.860 (3.13)*		-0.150 (0.46)	-20.390 (1.00)	Bahmani-Oskooee and Rehman's income elasticity for *M2* is 0.58.
Hussain et al., (2006)	*M0*	1972-2005	JML	0.752 (6.91)*	-0.060 (2.96)*		-0.032 (3.95)*	Hussain et al.,'s financial innovation estimate for *M0*, *M1*, *M2*, respectively, are -13.432, -16.289 and -11.169.
	M1	1972-2005	JML	0.740 (7.80)*	-0.079 (4.13)*		-0.035 (4.71)*	
	M2	1972-2005	JML	0.799 (6.98)*	-0.081 (3.81)*		-0.037 (4.54)*	
Papua New Guinea								
Kannapiran (2001)	*M2*	1979-1995	EG	0.200				
Valadkhani and Alauddin (2003)	*M2*	1979-2002	SUR	0.629 (7.50)*				
Philippines								
Valadkhani and Alauddin (2003)	*M2*	1979-1999	SUR	1.443 (7.60)*				
Bahmani-Oskooee and Rehman (2005)	*M1*	1973(Q1)-2000(Q4)	ARDL	0.300 (1.97)*		-0.040 (0.15)	-15.690 (1.99)*	Bahmani-Oskooee and Rehman's income elasticity for *M2* is 1.13.
Sierra Leone								
Valadkhani and Alauddin (2003)	*M2*	1979-1999	SUR	0.331 (1.90)**				

Country/Study	Money	Period	Method	ln*Y*	*R*	ln*E*	*P*	Remarks
Singapore								
Bahmani-Oskooee and Rehman (2005)	*M1*	1973(Q1)-2000(Q4)	ARDL	0.730 (13.78)*		-0.520 (3.07)*	-7.600 (3.59)*	The income elasticity for *M2* is 1.48
Somalia								
Arize et al., (1990)	*M1*	1960-1987	TSLS	0.490 (3.68)*			-0.310 (1.46)	Capital mobility estimate is -0.002.
South Africa					-2.760			
Wesso (2002)	*M3*	1971(Q1)-2000(Q4)	JML	1.840				*R* is the long term market interest rate. The short term interest rate spread estimate is -5.11.
Thailand					-0.009			
Dekle and Pradhan (1997)	*M1*	1978-1995	JML	1.130			0.670	Dekle and Pradhan used price level for *P*.
Valadkhani and Alauddin (2003)	*M2*	1979-1999	SUR	0.553 (6.00)*				
Bahmani-Oskooee and Rehman (2005)	*M1*	1973(Q1)-2000(Q4)	ARDL	0.140 (0.04)		2.570 (0.11)	-153.380 (0.13)	Bahmani-Oskooee and Rehman's income elasticity for *M2* is 0.90.

Chapter 4

EMPIRICAL RESULTS

4.1. INTRODUCTION

In this chapter, I have used the alternative time series techniques of GETS, FMOLS and JML to estimate the demand for narrow money for 15 developing countries viz,. Fiji (FJI), Vanuatu (VNT), Samoa (SAM), Solomon Islands (SOL), Tonga (TNG), India (IND), Indonesia (IDN), Philippines (PHL), Thailand (THA), Bangladesh (BGD), Kenya (KEN), Malawi (MWI), Jamaica (JAM), Rwanda (RWA) and South Africa (ZAF). We have also used Gregory and Hansen procedure to test for structural breaks in the cointegrating equation for demand for money for Fiji. Some of the countries like India and Indonesia are very large with a large volume of transactions and others like Fiji, Samoa, Solomon, Tonga and Vanuatu are small island countries. There are also medium sized countries like the Philippines, Bangladesh, Thailand, South Africa and Kenya. However, in terms of financial developments and general economic progress these countries are ranked equally. It would be interesting, therefore, to examine if the demand for money is influenced by the size of a country and the volume of transactions. This is of interest because, compared to the advanced countries with highly developed financial markets where cash is less frequently used in transactions, cash is often used as the medium of exchange in the day to day transactions in the developing countries.

Our objectives in this chapter are as follows. First, we estimate the income and interest rate elasticities and examine if they differ significantly across these countries. Second, we evaluate if the demand for money functions in these economies are stable because this has implications for the conduct of monetary policy. Third, we want to examine the demand for money function, particularly for Fiji, in the presence of structural breaks.

This chapter is organized as follows: Section 2 briefly discusses the money demand model and data. Section 3 details our alternative empirical results. Finally, Section 4 contains conclusions and policy implications.

4.2. Model and Data

We adopt the widely applied Keynesian specification of the demand for money in which demand for real narrow money is a function of real income and the nominal rate of interest. The interest rate measures the opportunity cost of holding money. Our basic specification is as follows:

$$\ln(M/P)_t = \beta_0 + \beta_1 \ln(Y/P)_t - \beta_2 R_t + \varepsilon_t \quad (1)$$

where M is nominal narrow money, P is the GDP deflator, Y is the nominal GDP measured at factor cost, R is the nominal weighted average interest rate on short-term deposits and ε is an *iid* error term. The demand for money is positively related to real income and negatively to the nominal rate of interest. Further, the demand for money is treated as the demand for real balances, implicitly assuming that the function is homogenous of degree one in the level of prices. We expect that the income elasticity is close to unity and the interest rate elasticity is significant with correct negative sign. However, in developed countries income elasticities are expected to be much lower than unity due to better financial systems. For a comprehensive survey of income elasticities for developed and less developed countries, see Sriram (1999).

This study is based on the annual data and sample periods are-- Fiji: 1971-2002, Vanuatu: 1978-2003, Samoa: 1982-2002, Solomon: 1978-2002, Tonga: 1978-2004, India:1973-2002, Philippines:1981-2004, Indonesia:1975-2004, Thailand: 1982-2004, Bangladesh: 1973-2003, Kenya:1971-2004, Jamaica: 1978-2003, Rwanda: 1984-2003, Malawi:1981-2004 and South Africa: 1970-2004. Definitions of the variables and sources of data are in Appendix (A). We tested for the presence of unit root in our variables. The Augmented Dicky-Fuller (ADF) test is used for testing for the order of the variables. The ADF test have been applied for both levels and their first differences with an intercept and trend. The time trend is included because it is significant in the levels and first differences of the variables. The computed test statistics for the levels and first differences of the variables are given in the Appendix (B). The null hypothesis of unit root cannot be rejected at the 5% level for the level variables ie. $\ln(M/P)_t$, $\ln(Y/P)_t$, and R_t. Alternatively, the null that their first differences have unit roots is clearly rejected. Therefore, the level variables are $I(1)$ and their first differences are stationary $I(0)$. There is no point in applying more sophisticated unit root tests because, compared to the ADF test, alternative unit root tests like the generalized least squares ADF test and the Elliott, Rothenburg and Stock test have more power against the unit root null.

4.3. Alternative Empirical Estimates

4.3.1. GETS, FMOLS and JML Estimates

I first report the cointegrating coefficients obtained with alternative approaches, see Table 1.[1] The GETS implied long run estimates are in the first three columns. The next three are for JML and FMOLS, respectively, which are obtained after subjecting the variables to unit root tests. The implied long run income (β_Y) and semi-interest rate elasticities (β_R) are similar for all countries across all the three approaches. Except for the Philippines where income elasticity is around 1.25, we obtained close to unit income elasticities for all other countries. The Wald tests on the null of unit income elasticities were not rejected at 5% for all countries. The Wald test results are not reported to conserve space.

The implied semi-interest rate elasticities vary from country to country, but they have the expected negative sign and are significant. The sample average of the implied long run interest rate elasticities (at their mean rates) are; -0.256 in GETS, -0.369 in JML and -0.298 in FMOLS. These results are comparable to Sriram (1999) for developing countries, Bahmani-Oskooee and Rehman(2005) for Asian economies, Rao and Singh (2005a and 2005c) for Fiji and India, Pradhan and Subramanian (2003) for India and Hafer and Kutan (2003) for Philippines.

---

[1] In the parentheses are the absolute *t*-ratios and * and ** indicates significance at 5% and 10% levels, respectively. The income (β_Y) and semi-interest rate (β_R) elasticities are significant at 5%. However, in JML β_R for SOL and MWI are significant at 10% level and in GETS β_R for IND is significant at 10% level. Sample periods are; FJI:1971-2002, VNT:1978-2003, SAM: 1982-2002, SOL:1978-2002, TNG:1978-2004, BGD: 1973-2003, IND:1973-2002, PHL:1981-2002, IDN:1975-2004, THA:1982-2004, KEN:1971-2004, JAM:1978-2003, RWA:1984-2003, MWI:1981-2004 and ZAF:1970-2004. Based on Ericsson and MacKinnon (2002), the null of no cointegration was rejected at 5% in GETS and FMOLS for all the countries. Nevertheless, the Eigenvalue and Trace tests in JML indicated cointegration for all countries at conventional levels. Details of these tests are available from the authors.

Table 1. Alternative Estimates of Equilibrium Elasticities

	GETS	JML	FMOLS
	$\beta_0 \beta_R \beta_Y$	$\beta_0 \beta_R \beta_Y$	$\beta_0 \beta_R \beta_Y$
FJI	-1.28 -0.03 0.93 (0.84) (3.58)* (4.73)*	-0.05 1.06 (3.61)* (4.38)*	-1.20 -0.05 0.96 (1.25) (5.90)* (7.68)*
VNT	4.16 -0.01 0.91 (147.5)* (2.53)* (7.18)*	4.51 -0.01 0.93 (12.45)* (2.04)* (12.41)*	4.42 -0.01 0.94 (20.12)* (2.85)* (20.68)*
SAM	0.11 -0.11 0.97 (0.05) (3.62)* (2.80)*	-0.11 1.01 (10.17)* (48.37)*	0.11 -0.11 0.97 (0.19) (16.27)* (7.55)*
SOL	0.08 -0.05 1.13 (0.81) (2.73)* (6.04)*	-0.05 1.18 (1.93)** (32.37)*	0.13 -0.04 1.18 (0.07) (3.53)* (2.87)*
TNG	4.61 -0.04 1.17 (4.50)* (4.99)* (2.05)*	-0.04 1.05 (2.57)* (11.53)*	0.89 -0.07 0.96 (0.11) (2.27)* (13.01)*
IND	-8.32 -0.03 1.17 (15.41)* (1.78)** (24.48)*	-7.92 -0.02 1.13 (20.23)* (1.99)* (37.12)*	-7.66 -0.02 1.11 (28.97)* (2.55)* (51.07)*
PHL	0.45 -0.04 1.24 (0.86) (7.01)* (11.57)*	0.47 -0.05 1.25 (0.47) (2.77)* (6.87)*	0.68 -0.05 1.21 (2.06)* (14.88)* (17.39)*
THA	1.63 -0.03 1.09 (5.42)* (4.80)* (17.88)*	1.93 -0.04 1.02 (5.56)* (4.68)* (14.15)*	1.67 -0.04 1.06 (29.52)* (29.28)* (90.70)*
IDN	7.23 -0.01 1.01 (64.60)* (2.32)* (36.61)*	6.54 -0.01 1.12 (19.10)* (2.48)* (22.18)*	7.39 -0.01 1.01 (157.2)* (10.40)* (82.48)*
BGD	2.96 -0.04 0.99 (8.46)* (2.74)* (12.75)*	-0.04 1.07 (2.45)* (12.68)*	2.16 -0.02 1.03 (1.45) (2.55)* (3.98)*
KEN	2.97 -0.03 1.04 (27.15)* (2.59)* (7.93)*	-0.10 1.27 (2.09)* (7.26)*	3.05 -0.02 1.09 (22.40)* (2.49)* (16.73)*
JAM	5.56 -0.01 1.14 (11.14)* (2.00)* (9.59)*	6.02 -0.01 1.03 (21.67)* (2.45)* (16.42)*	6.12 -0.01 1.01 (44.24)* (6.36)* (32.49)*
RWA	1.89 -0.03 1.00 (60.95)* (3.65)* (2.55)*	-0.07 1.02 (6.29)* (20.81)*	2.09 -0.09 1.09 (7.14)* (9.40)* (16.30)*
MWI	1.26 -0.01 1.07 (0.17) (2.51)* (21.82)*	-0.01 1.06 (1.89)** (43.07)*	0.04 -0.01 1.02 (0.15) (2.10)* (17.86)*
ZAF	3.21 -0.06 0.92 (0.62) (3.27)* (2.54)*	-0.09 1.13 (2.10)* (2.39)*	4.56 -0.03 1.18 (1.22) (4.89)* (10.23)*

However, as is required, we subjected the cointegrating coefficients reported for JML to further tests. The identification tests indicate that all the implied long run relations represent demand for money functions, since only the one period lagged residuals normalized on money ($ECMM_t$) were significant with correct negative signs in $\Delta\ln(M/P)_t$ equations. Both the residuals normalized on income $ECMY_{t-1}$ and the rate of interest $ECMR_{t-1}$ were insignificant in their respective regressions. The computed ECM coefficients and their *t*-ratios in parenthesis for each country are reported in the diagonal of their respective (3×3) matrices in Appendix, see Table-C(i) and C(ii).

Further, following Enders (2004) another set of three ECM equations for each country were estimated with their respective $ECMM_{t-1}$ being included as one of the independent variables in each of the implied equations. The $ECMM_{t-1}$ was only significant in equations where the dependent variables were $\Delta\ln(M/P)_t$ in all cases. The exogeneity test results are also in Table-C(i) and C(ii), see along the first row in each matrix. Since the dis-equilibrium in the respective money markets does not significantly contribute to the explanation of $\ln(Y/P)_t$ and R_t in all cases, we treated $\ln(Y/P)_t$ and R_t as being weakly exogenous in all the respective money demand equations.

Using the one period lagged residuals from the above cointegrating relations, the dynamic money demand equations for each country were estimated with JML and FMOLS. We used the General to Specific approach to search for the best lag structure. Note in GETS, both the equilibrium relation and the dynamics are estimated in one step. However, it is not pragmatic to report all estimates based on the three approaches and consequently, we have only reported the JML dynamic specifications in Table-2(a-d) as JML seems to be the widely used approach in applied works. This does not imply that JML is superior to others. The dynamic estimates in GETS and FMOLS are comparable to JML and in some cases gave marginally better results.[2] In all these tables, the absolute *t*-ratios are below the coefficients and *p*-values for X^2 tests are reported in parentheses. The X^2_{sc}, X^2_{ff}, X^2_n and X^2_{hs} are test statistics for the null of no serial correlation, functional form mis-specification, normality of residuals and heteroscedasticity, respectively. * and ** denotes significance at 5% and 10% levels, respectively and (c) is the constraint estimate. Table-2(a) includes estimates for Fiji Vanuatu, Philippines and Solomons. Their unconstraint estimates are given as (i) and with some coefficient restrictions, we obtained their preferred equations reported as (ii).[3] For Fiji, *DUM1* captures the effects of the two political instabilities of 1987 and 2000.[4] It has a positive coefficient because the coup is likely to increase holdings of precautionary balances. *DUM2* resembles the combined effect of two devaluations (in 1987 and 1998) and the NBF crisis (in 1996) in Fiji

[2] These are available from the authors upon request.

[3] For instance, for Fiji the coefficients of $ln(Y/P)_{t-4}$, $\Delta ln(M/P)_{t-1}$ and *DUM1* are close and the Wald test computed $X^2_{(1)}$ test statistic with *p*-value in parenthesis is 1.957 (0.162) is insignificant and therefore the constraint could not be rejected. For Vanuatu, the coefficients of $\Delta ln(Y/P)_{t-1}$ and $\Delta ln(Y/P)_{t-2}$ are close and Wald test could not reject the constraint ($X^2_{(1)}$ test statistic with *p*-value in parenthesis is 0.09 (0.76)). Similarly for Philippines the coefficients of $\Delta ln(Y/P)_t$ and $\Delta ln(Y/P)_{t-2}$ are close and the Wald test computed $X^2_{(1)}$ test statistic with *p*-value in parenthesis is 0.807(0.369) is insignificant.

[4] *DUM1* is a dummy variable for Fiji and is constructed as 1 in 1987 and 2000 and zero otherwise.

which has negative effects. For Vanuatu and Philippines, *DUM2* represents the financial sector reforms which has positive impact as better and efficient financial systems allow improved availability of credit.[5]

Table 2(b) shows the dynamic estimates for Samoa, Jamaica, Thailand and Indonesia. Their initial parsimonious versions (unconstraint estimates) are given as (i). The constraint versions are our preferred equations reported as (ii).[6] Table 2(c) reports the results for India, Rwanda and Kenya. These have shorter dynamic structures but the estimates are quite reasonable. In some of these, notably, India and Thailand, the lagged growth of inflation rates (Δ^2 ln*P*) seems to be significant. For Rwanda, *DUM* represents the financial sector reforms and has positive effects on demand for money.[7] We also tested for parameter constraints for India and Rwanda.[8] Thus our preferred equations for India and Rwanda are reported as (ii). Table 2(d) shows the estimates for Bangladesh, South Africa, Tonga and Malawi. In all cases the growth in expected inflation seems to have temporary negative effects on demand for money. The *DUM* for Bangladesh captures the effects of financial reforms and found to have significant positive impact on money demand.[9] It is noteworthy that Tonga has some parameter restrictions.[10] The constraint version is given by (ii).

---

[5] *DUM2* for Fiji is constructed as 1 in 1987 and 1996-1998 and zero in other periods. *DUM2* for Vanuatu and Philippines are constructed as 1 from 1980-2000 and zero otherwise.

[6] For Samoa, the coefficients of ΔR_t and ΔR_{t-1} are close and the Wald test could not reject this restriction ($X^2_{(1)}$ test statistic with *p*-value in parenthesis is 0.49 (0.48)). Also for Samoa, the estimates of $\Delta ln(M/P)_{t-1}$ and $\Delta ln(M/P)_{t-3}$ are close and restriction was also accepted by the Wald test because $X^2_{(1)}$ test statistic with *p*-value in parenthesis is 0.43 (0.51) is insignificant. For Jamaica, the coefficients of ΔR_{t-1} and ΔR_{t-1} are close and the Wald test $X^2_{(1)}$ test statistic with *p*-value in parenthesis is 1.02 (0.31) is insignificant. For Thailand, the coefficients of ΔR_t and ΔR_{t-2} are close and the Wald test could not reject the constraint beacuse its $X^2_{(1)}$ test statistic with *p*-value in parenthesis is 0.20 (0.65) is insignificant. For Indonesia, the coefficients of ΔR_t and ΔR_{t-1} are close and the constraint was accepted by the Wald test ($X^2_{(1)}$ test statistic with *p*-value in parenthesis is 0.76 (0.13)).

[7] *DUM* for Rwanda is constructed as 1 from 1985-1995 and zero otherwise.

[8] For India, the coefficients of $\Delta^2\ lnP_{t-1}$ and $\Delta^2\ lnP_{t-2}$ are close and the constraint was not rejected by the Wald test because its $X^2_{(1)}$ test statistic with *p*-value in parenthesis is 0.89 (0.35). Similarly, for Rwanda the coefficients of $\Delta ln(Y/P)_{t-1}$ and $\Delta ln(Y/P)_{t-2}$ are close and the Wald test could not reject the restriction. Further, the coefficients ΔR_{t-1} and ΔR_{t-2} were also restricted for Rwanda. For Rwanda, the Wald test $X^2_{(1)}$ test statistics with *p*-values in parenthesis for both constraints, respectively, are 0.20(0.65) and 0.16(0.69).

[9] *DUM* for Bangladesh is constructed as 1 from 1980-1985 and zero in other periods.

[10] The coefficients of $\Delta \ln(Y/P)_{t-2}$, $\Delta \ln(Y/P)_{t-4}$ and $\Delta^2\ \ln P_{t-1}$ are close and Wald test $X^2_{(1)}$ test statistics with *p*-value in parenthesis is 0.31(0.12) is insignificant and the restriction could not be rejected. Likewise the coefficients of ΔR_t and ΔR_{t-3} are close and restriction was accepted by the Wald test because its $X^2_{(1)}$ test statistics with *p*-value in parenthesis is 0.87(0.45) is insignificant and the restriction could not be rejected.

Note for all the dynamic estimates reported in Tables-2(a-d), the X^2 summary statistics are insignificant at 5% level. For Fiji, Kenya and Thailand the functional form is significant at 10% but not at 5% level. The *SERs* in all estimates are low and the ECM_{t-1} terms are strongly significant with correct negative signs implying negative feedback mechanisms in all dynamic equations. The fit of the actual vs. predicted values of growth of real *M1* gives fairly high adjusted R^2 and lower *SERs* for all (except for Jamaica). The slope is close to unity and the constant term is zero.

To shed additional light on the relationship between real narrow money, real income and nominal interest rate, this study also applies structural stability tests including the *CUSUM* and the *CUSUM SQUARES* procedures developed by Brown et al. (1975).

The *CUSUM* procedure is based on the cumulative recursive sum of recursive residuals. However, the *CUSUM SQUARES* framework is based on the cumulative sum of squares of recursive residuals. To draw inferences relative to the stability of the parameters and the model in particular, the *CUSUM* and the *CUSUM SQUARES* procedures are updated recursively and are plotted against the break points.

The null hypothesis of instability is rejected when the plots of the *CUSUM* and the *CUSUM SQUARES* stay within the 5 percent significance level. However, the model is unstable when the plots of the *CUSUM* and the *CUSUM SQUARES* move outside the 5 percent critical lines. Both the *CUSUM* and the *CUSUM SQUARES* stability tests were applied to all preferred dynamic equations. The JML based plots of only *CUSUM SQUARES* are presented in the Appendix (The plot of *CUSUM* is not reported to conserve space). As can be seen from the Figures, the plots for *CUSUM SQUARES* remained within the 5 percent critical bounds. This finding suggests that the demand for money functions in all our selected developing countries is stable.

Table 2(a). JML Dynamic Adjustment Equations

	FJI (i)	FJI(ii)	VNT(i)	VNT(ii)	PHL(i)	PHL(ii)	SOL(i)	SOL(ii)
Intercept	-2.676 (6.05)*	-2.477 (7.31)*	-0.013 (0.75)	-0.013 (0.77)	-0.026 (1.12)	-0.026 (1.16)	0.307 (3.89)*	0.306 (4.03)*
ECM_{t-1}	-1.306 (6.06)*	-1.211 (7.39)*	-1.313 (6.20)*	-1.312 (6.39)*	-0.532 (3.35)*	-0.498 (4.53)*	-0.079 (3.49)*	-0.079 (3.64)*
$\Delta\ln(Y/P)_t$			0.851 (6.56)*	0.853 (6.89)*	0.919 (1.75)**	1.050 (3.53)*	1.970 (4.05)*	1.973 (4.20)*
$\Delta\ln(Y/P)_{t-1}$	-2.266 (5.58)*	-2.244 (6.26)*	-0.141 (1.06)	-0.146 (1.80)**				
$\Delta\ln(Y/P)_{t-2}$	-0.789 (1.90)**	-0.711 (1.95)**	-0.151 (1.13)	-0.146 (c)	1.194 (2.14)*	1.050 (c)	-1.173 (2.60)*	-1.128 (2.93)*
$\Delta\ln(Y/P)_{t-4}$	0.568 (1.92)**	0.251 (6.94)*					-1.034 (1.75)**	-1.128 (c)
ΔR_t	-0.049 (3.40)*	-0.040 (5.12)*			-0.037 (5.57)*	-0.034 (7.44)*		
ΔR_{t-1}	0.035 (2.90)*	0.040 (c)						
ΔR_{t-3}							-0.078 (3.49)*	-0.079 (c)
$\Delta\ln(M/P)_{t-1}$	0.274 (1.74)**	0.251 (6.94)*					-0.272 (1.63)	-0.268 (1.67)**
DUM1	0.261 (6.79)*	0.251 (c)						
DUM2	-0.054 (2.43)*	-0.048 (2.33)*	0.113 (2.33)*	0.113 (2.39)*	0.132 (2.80)*	0.130 (2.84)*		

	FJI (i)	FJI(ii)	VNT(i)	VNT(ii)	PHL(i)	PHL(ii)	SOL(i)	SOL(ii)
Adjusted R^2	0.803	0.816	0.776	0.788	0.720	0.732	0.535	0.566
SEE	0.065	0.063	0.077	0.075	0.072	0.069	0.084	0.081
X^2_{sc}	0.324 (0.57)	0.676 (0.41)	0.893 (0.35)	0.858 (0.35)	0.952 (0.33)	0.920 (0.59)	1.291 (0.26)	1.031 (0.31)
X^2_{ff}	3.325 (0.07)**	3.063 (0.08)**	0.259 (0.61)	0.262 (0.61)	0.324 (0.57)	0.290 (0.59)	0.015 (0.90)	0.050 (0.82)
X^2_{n}	0.371 (0.83)	0.500 (0.78)	1.085 (0.58)	1.071 (0.59)	0.155 (0.93)	0.322 (0.85)	0.545 (0.76)	0.640 (0.73)
X^2_{hs}	0.020 (0.89)	0.025 (0.90)	0.006 (0.94)	0.007 (0.93)	0.998 (0.32)	1.000 (0.32)	0.139 (0.71)	0.110 (0.74)

Table 2(b). JML Dynamic Adjustment Equations

	SAM(i)	SAM(ii)	JAM(i)	JAM(ii)	THA(i)	THA(ii)	IDN(i)	IDN(ii)
Intercept	0.085 (2.88)*	0.089 (3.69)*	-0.011 (0.23)	-0.010 (0.22)	1.378 (6.35)*	1.358 (5.67)*	0.179 (2.30)*	0.179 (2.34)*
Trend			0.004 (1.30)	0.004 (1.30)				
ECM_{t-1}	-0.857 (18.09)*	-0.850 (20.49)*	-1.126 (4.96)*	-1.105 (5.07)*	-0.682 (6.03)*	-0.667 (6.32)*	-0.390 (2.52)*	-0.389 (2.61)*
$\Delta\ln(Y/P)_t$					1.997 (6.84)*	2.030 (7.28)*	1.359 (5.39)*	1.358 (8.77)*
$\Delta\ln(Y/P)_{t-1}$					-2.190 (6.21)*	-2.309 (7.74)*		
ΔR_t	-0.073 (3.28)*	-0.065 (4.86)*			-0.013 (1.83)**	-0.009 (2.41)*	-0.005 (1.86)**	-0.005 (3.61)*
ΔR_{t-1}	0.060 (3.00)*	-0.065 (c)	0.005 (1.14)	0.007 (1.83)**			0.005 (1.93)**	0.005 (c)
ΔR_{t-2}	0.048 (2.37)*	0.045 (2.62)*	0.008 (1.78)**	0.007 (c)	0.008 (1.49)	0.009 (c)		
ΔR_{t-3}			0.009 (2.04)*	0.008 (2.36)*				
$\Delta\ln(M/P)_{t-1}$	-0.151 (2.41)*	-0.176 (4.81)*						
$\Delta\ln(M/P)_{t-2}$	-0.210 (3.25)*	-0.219 (4.11)*						

	SAM(i)	SAM(ii)	JAM(i)	JAM(ii)	THA(i)	THA(ii)	IDN(i)	IDN(ii)
$\Delta\ln(M/P)_{t-3}$	-0.186 (3.04)*	-0.176 (c)						
Adjusted R^2	0.951	0.957	0.487	0.508	0.833	0.842	0.751	0.760
SEE	0.097	0.091	0.080	0.079	0.061	0.052	0.065	0.064
X^2_{sc}	0.102 (0.75)	0.000 (0.99)	0.134 (0.72)	0.099 (0.75)	1.099 (0.29)	2.047 (0.15)	0.001 (0.99)	0.001 (0.99)
X^2_{ff}	1.627 (0.20)	1.905 (0.17)	2.509 (0.11)	2.343 (0.13)	3.734 (0.05)*	3.453 (0.06)**	0.092 (0.76)	0.089 (0.77)
X^2_{n}	0.420 (0.81)	0.531 (0.77)	0.050 (0.98)	0.082 (0.96)	3.282 (0.19)	2.923 (0.23)	0.591 (0.74)	0.595 (0.74)
X^2_{hs}	0.696 (0.40)	0.714 (0.40)	0.120 (0.66)	0.225 (0.64)	1.168 (0.68)	1.115 (0.73)	0.643 (0.42)	0.643 (0.42)

Table 2(c). JML Dynamic Adjustment Equations

	IND (i)	IND(ii)	RWA(i)	RWA(ii)	KEN(i)
Intercept	0.026 (0.87)	0.026 (0.88)	3.573 (5.17)*	3.408 (5.38)*	0.291 (2.02)*
Trend	0.001 (1.29)	0.001 (1.32)	-0.010 (1.83)**	-0.009 (1.68)**	
ECM_{t-1}	-0.460 (3.14)*	-0.457 (3.23)*	-1.608 (5.14)*	-1.461 (5.34)*	-1.105 (2.10)*
$\Delta\ln(Y/P)_t$	0.625 (2.82)*	0.630 (2.94)*			1.054 (7.62)*
$\Delta\ln(Y/P)_{t-1}$			-1.009 (4.17)*	-0.851 (4.59)*	
$\Delta\ln(Y/P)_{t-2}$			-0.844 (4.18)*	0.851 (c)	
ΔR_{t-1}	0.015 (2.00)*	0.016 (2.10)*	0.086 (4.35)*	0.080 (4.57)*	0.613 (1.76)**
ΔR_{t-2}			0.094 (3.91)*	0.080 (c)	
$\Delta\ln(M/P)_{t-2}$			1.344 (4.41)*	1.274 (4.49)*	
$\Delta^2 \ln P_{t-1}$	-0.351 (2.62)*	-0.361 (3.65)*	-1.510 (4.58)*	-1.461 (4.99)*	
$\Delta^2 \ln P_{t-2}$	-0.368 (3.15)*	-0.361 (c)			
DUM1			0.490 (4.34)*	0.435 (4.46)*	
Adjusted R^2	0.520	0.540	0.542	0.572	0.647
SEE	0.029	0.028	0.066	0.064	0.095
X^2_{sc}	0.014 (0.91)	0.002 (0.97)	1.641 (0.20)	1.445 (0.23)	0.727 (0.39)
X^2_{ff}	2.621 (0.11)	2.515 (0.11)	0.013 (0.91)	0.024 (0.88)	2.959 (0.09)**
X^2_n	1.320 (0.52)	1.414 (0.49)	0.735 (0.69)	0.981 (0.61)	1.808 (0.41)
X^2_{hs}	0.132 (0.72)	0.115 (0.74)	0.408 (0.52)	0.320 (0.57)	0.307 (0.58)

Table 2(d). JML Dynamic Adjustment Equations

	BGD(i)	ZAF(i)	TNG(i)	TNG(ii)	MWI(i)
Intercept	0.791 (3.36)*	2.339 (2.11)*	0.081 (2.03)*	0.086 (2.55)*	0.003 (2.15)*
ECM_{t-1}	-0.208 (3.28)*	-0.324 (5.67)*	-0.146 (4.04)*	-0.141 (4.05)*	-0.235 (5.67)*
$\Delta\ln(M/P)_{t-1}$	-0.666 (3.74)*				-1.398 (2.38)*
$\Delta\ln(Y/P)_{t-2}$		0.398 (2.89)*	1.170 (2.88)*	1.103 (3.57)*	
$\Delta\ln(Y/P)_{t-4}$			-1.061 (2.60)*	-1.103 (c)	
ΔR_t	-0.043 (2.91)*		0.141 (2.35)*	0.140 (3.02)*	2.670 (3.56)*
ΔR_{t-2}	0.068 (3.98)*	0.231 (1.89)**			
ΔR_{t-3}		-1.335 (2.11)*	0.138 (2.35)*	0.140 (c)	
$\Delta^2 \ln P_t$	-0.808 (5.46)*	-1.417 (3.53)*			-0.563 (3.21)*
$\Delta^2 \ln P_{t-1}$	-0.137 (1.87)**		-1.061 (2.19)*	-1.103 (c)	
DUM	0.130 (2.29)*				
Adjusted R^2	0.747	0.716	0.542	0.572	0.627
SEE	0.062	0.028	0.066	0.064	0.032
X^2_{sc}	2.285 (0.13)	0.006 (0.87)	1.641 (0.20)	1.445 (0.23)	1.296 (0.26)
X^2_{ff}	1.196 (0.27)	2.675 (0.18)	0.013 (0.91)	0.024 (0.88)	1.380 (0.24)
X^2_n	0.405 (0.82)	1.234 (0.69)	0.735 (0.69)	0.981 (0.61)	0.631 (0.43)
X^2_{hs}	0.140 (0.71)	0.125 (0.44)	0.408 (0.52)	0.320 (0.57)	0.165 (0.69)

4.3.2. Structural Breaks and Money Demand: Case of FIJI

In what follows, we examine the stability of demand for money only in Fiji with the Gregory and Hansen (1996a) technique which allows for structural breaks in the cointegrating relationship. The implied specifications for the three Gregory and Hansen equations with structural breaks are as follows.[1]

$$\ln M_t = \mu_1 + \mu_2 \varphi_{tk} + \alpha_1 \ln Y_t - \alpha_2 r_t + \varepsilon_t \quad (2)$$

$$\ln M_t = \mu_1 + \mu_2 \varphi_{tk} + \beta_1 t + \alpha_1 \ln Y_t - \alpha_2 r_t + \varepsilon_t \quad (3)$$

$$\ln M_t = \mu_1 + \mu_2 \varphi_{tk} + \beta_1 t + \alpha_1 \ln Y_t + \alpha_{11} \ln Y_t \varphi_{tk} - \alpha_2 r_t - \alpha_{22} r_t \varphi_{tk} + \varepsilon_t \quad (4)$$

where M is real narrow money, Y is real GDP and r is the nominal rate of interest. For convenience these equations will be referred as GH-I, GH-II and GH-III respectively. Our sample period for Fiji is from 1971 to 2002 but due to the presence of some lagged variables, the three aforesaid structural break models (equations (2) to (4)) are estimated from 1974 to 2002 and the results are given below in Table-3.

Table 3. Tests for Cointegration with Structural Breaks 1974-2002

	Brake Date	GH Test Statistic	5% Critical Value	Reject H_0 of no Cointegration
GH-I	1987	-5.384	-4.92	YES
GH-II	1976	-5.483	-5.29	YES
GH-III	1987	-6.290	-5.50	YES

These results, which are self-explanatory, imply that irrespective of which of the three models with structural breaks is used, there is a cointegrating relation between real money, real income and the nominal rate of interest in Fiji. However, the endogenously determined brake date is 1987 in GH-I and GH-III, but different at 1976 in GH-II. Since the null is rejected by all the three models, it is hard to decide which is the best. Therefore, we have estimated the cointegrating equations for the three models with the Engle-Granger method and the first stage OLS equations are given below in Table-4.

From these estimates it can be said that GH-I is the most plausible model. In this model all the estimated coefficients, except the pre 1987 intercept, are significant and their values are plausible although the estimate of income elasticity at 0.76 seems to be a bit low.

[1] The fourth model developed by Gregory and Hansen (1996b) is
$\ln M_t = \mu_1 + \mu_2 \varphi_{tk} + \beta_1 t + \beta_2 t\varphi_{tk} + \alpha_1 \ln Y_t + \alpha_{11} \ln Y_t \varphi_{tk} - \alpha_2 r_t - \alpha_{22} r_t \varphi_{tk} + \varepsilon_t$
We ignore this model in this thesis because of some limitations in our software.

Table 4. Cointegrating Equations 1974-2002[2]

	GII-I	GH-II	GH-III
Intercept	0.283 (0.27)	1.387 (4.29)*	2.300 (2.83)*
Trend		0.022 (3.11)*	
$\ln Y_t$	0.760 (4.29)*	0.328 (1.08)	-0.531 (1.29)
r_t	-0.035 (4.37)*	-0.018 (4.20)*	-0.001 (0.52)
Dummy 1976		-0.200 (1.53)	
Dummy 1987	0.221 (3.96)*		1.280 (2.39)*
Dummy 1987 $\times \ln Y_t$			0.028 (1.22)
Dummy 1987 $\times r_t$			0.109 (2.11)*

However, the Wald test could not reject the null that it is unity at the 5% level. The computed test statistic, with its p-value in brackets, is 1.462 (0.227). In GH-II the estimate of income elasticity is low at 0.3 and insignificant. In GH-III the income elasticity is negative and statistically insignificant. The results in GH-II and GH-III can be rejected as implausible. Therefore, we shall use the residuals from GH-I to estimate the short run dynamic equation for the demand for money with the error-correction adjustment model (ECM).

In developing an appropriate ECM model for the short run, we adopted the LSE-Hendry's GETS approach in the second stage. This second stage equation is estimated with OLS in which $\Delta\ln M_t$ is regressed on its lagged values, the current and lagged values of $\Delta\ln Y_t$ and Δr_t and the one period lagged residuals from the cointegrating vector of Gregory and Hansen i.e., from equation GH-I. We have used lags up to 4 periods and using the variable deletion tests in Microfit 4.1 and arrived at the following parsimonious equation:

$$\Delta\ln M_t = -0.192\, ECM_{t-1} + 1.038\, \Delta\ln Y_t - 0.794\, \Delta\ln Y_{t-1}$$
$$(1.92)^{**}\ (2.87)^{*}\ (1.91)^{**}$$
$$+ 0.025\, \Delta^2 r_{t-1}$$
$$(2.42)^{*} \qquad (5)$$

[2] Absolute t-ratios are reported below the coefficients. * indicates significance at 5% level.

$\bar{R}^2 = 0.563$, $SER = 0.098$, *Period*: 1975-2002
$X^2_{sc1} = 0.748\ (0.21)$, $X^2_{ff} = 1.290\ (0.04)^*$,
$X^2_{n} = 0.279\ (0.27)$, $X^2_{hs} = 3.156\ (0.05)^*$

where * and ** indicate significance at the 5% and 10% levels, respectively. It may be noted from these estimates that it is possible to reduce further the number of estimated coefficients to increase the degrees of freedom. The coefficients of $\Delta\ln Y_t$ and $\Delta\ln Y_{t-1}$ are close and opposite in sign. When this restriction is tested, the Wald test computed $\chi^2(1)$ test statistic with p value in the parenthesis is 0.157 (0.172) is insignificant and the constraint could not be rejected. The following ultra parsimonious equation is based on this restriction:

$$\begin{aligned}\Delta\ln M_t = &-0.374\, ECM_{t-1} + 0.836\, \Delta^2 \ln Y_{t-1} \\ &(1.76)^{**} \quad (5.38)^* \\ &+ 0.021\, \Delta^2 r_{t-1} \\ &(2.94)^* \end{aligned} \qquad (6)$$

$\bar{R}^2 = 0.583$, $SER = 0.097$, *Period*: 1975-2002
$X^2_{sc1} = 0.831\ (0.39)$, $X^2_{ff} = 2.110\ (0.04)^*$,
$X^2_{n} = 2.733\ (0.60)$, $X^2_{hs} = 1.233\ (0.32)$

The summary statistics of this equation have marginally improved. All the estimated coefficients are significant. The coefficient of the lagged error correction term is significant at 10% level with correct negative sign, and serves as the expected negative feedback function. This implies that if there are departures from equilibrium in the previous period, this departure is reduced by about 40% in the current period. The χ^2 statistics indicate that there is no serial correlation (χ^2_{sc1}), non-normality (χ^2_{n}) and heteroscedasticity (χ^2_{hs}) in the residuals. However, it may be noted that the functional form misspecification χ^2_{ff} test is marginally significant at the 5% but not at 1% level. This is not unusual for dynamic equations because it is hard to claim that the complex nature of dynamic adjustments, with limited data, can be adequately captured with linear specifications.

Having obtained the long run equilibrium estimates and the dynamic counterpart, we subjected our preferred Equation (6) to *CUSUM* and *CUSUM SQUARES* stability tests and neither the *CUSUM* nor the *CUSUM SQUARES* showed any instability. The plot of *CUSUM SQUARES* is given in Figure 1.[3] It shows that the money demand function is temporally stable in Fiji.

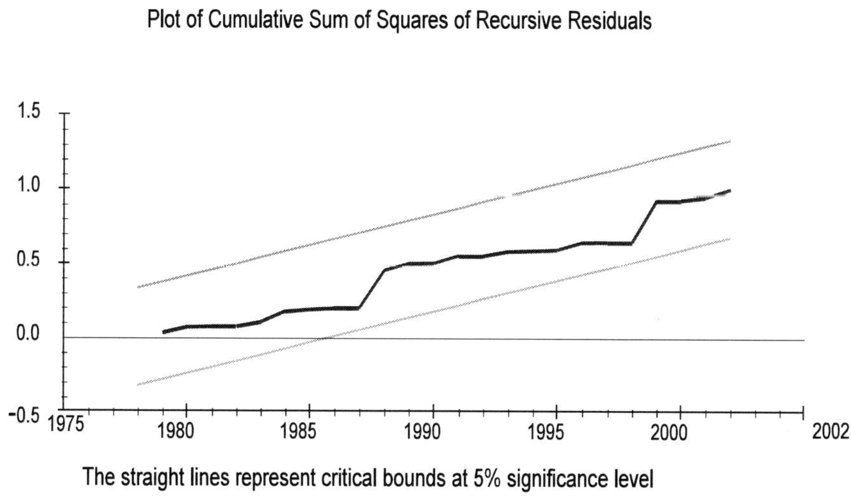

Figure 1. Cusum Squares Test for Equation 6.

Conclusions and Policy Implications

In this chapter, I have applied alternative time series methods to estimate demand for money in selected developing countries from the South Pacific, Asian and African regions and made the following observations. First, all the approaches, GETS, JML and FMOLS yielded similar cointegrating coefficients although their dynamic adjustment lags are somewhat different. I argue that when alternative time series techniques are implemented properly, it is likely they will give similar cointegration results. However, we must recognize the purpose of research and interpretation of results and it is pointless to emphasize the superiority of the estimation methods.

Results show the income elasticities are unity in all the three approaches for all countries in our sample, except for the Philippines where it is slightly higher at 1.25, and the interest rate elasticities are small, but significant and negative varying across countries. I also found that there were no significant differences between the income and interest rate elasticities of large and smaller developing countries. Thus, I found that the demand for money in these countries are stable and therefore, following Poole (1970), money supply

[3] The plot of *CUSUM* test is not presented to conserve space.

is the appropriate monetary policy instrument for central banks in these countries. In case of Fiji, I have also used the Gregory and Hansen procedure to test the stability of the demand for money. Our estimates imply that there exist a cointegrating relationship between real money, real income and nominal rate of interest which might have shifted up by about 0.23 after the 1987 coup. However, the major finding is that there exists a stable demand for money in Fiji even in the presence of structural breaks in the model.

Chapter 5

CONCLUSIONS AND LIMITATIONS

5.1. CONCLUSIONS

In this book, I have briefly reviewed the literature on demand for money in the industrial and developing countries. I noted that most of these studies seems to have drawbacks in their specification and as a result the implied income elasticity of money demand is either over-estimated or under-estimated. Another reason for implausible estimates in existing studies could be the limitations in data. Further, I have discussed the theories of demand for money developed by Keynes and Friedman. The Keynesian developed liquidity preference theory in which he distinguished three motives for holding money- transactions, precautionary and speculative. Alternatively, Friedman developed modern quantity theory in which money is assumed to be abstract purchasing power.

I have applied alternative time series methods to estimate demand for money in selected developing countries from the South Pacific, Asian and African regions and made the following observations. First all the approaches, GETS, JML and FMOLS gave similar and consistent cointegrating coefficients for all the countries, although their dynamic adjustments were somewhat different. Thus, it is highly unlikely that when implemented properly, alternative methods will give conflicting results. Second, not withstanding the relative merits/demerits of each approach, one should adopt a method that is simple to implement and gives reasonable summaries of observed facts. In this respect, we must not lose sight of the purpose of research and interpretation of results and avoid emphasizing the superiority of estimation methods. Third, the results show that the estimated income and interest rate elasticities are well-determined and their signs and magnitudes are consistent with *prior* expectations. The income elasticities are unity in all the three approaches for all countries in our sample, except for the Philippines where it is slightly higher at 1.25, and the interest rate elasticities are small, but significant and negative varying across countries. Fourthly, I noted that there were no major differences between the income and interest rate elasticities of large and smaller developing countries. Finally, I found that demand for money in these countries are stable. Therefore, money supply is the appropriate monetary policy instrument for central banks in these countries.

In addition, I have used the Gregory and Hansen procedure to test the stability of the demand for money only for Fiji. Our estimates imply that there exists a cointegrating relationship between real money, real income and nominal rate of interest which might have shifted up by about 0.23 after the 1987 coup in Fiji. This may be due to some increased precautionary demand for liquidity. However, the major finding is that there is a well-determined and stable demand for money in Fiji from 1971 to 2002. Further, our Gregory and Hansen estimates imply that the income elasticity of 0.758 is, although somewhat lower than unity, but the Wald test indicates that our estimate is not significantly different from unity. The estimate of interest rate elasticity, at its mean value of 6.97%, is about –0.244 and consistent with the GETS, FMOLS and JML findings.

5.2. LIMITATIONS

There are few limitations in this work. First, given the scope of this book, I am unable to extend this work in the lines of forecasting and policy analysis. Second, I have ignored structural breaks and their implications for other countries in the sample. I argue that there are practical problems in utilizing the break point test such as Gregory and Hansen when there are only a limited number of annual observations for developing countries. Nonetheless, I consider that structural change methodology is useful and should be adopted in estimating long run relationships for countries facing frequent instabilities. Thus I have used the usual *TIMVAR* stability tests in all cases which suggest that all the estimated equations are stable. I am hopeful that this work will be useful starting point for further works and may encourage other researchers to work on similar lines for other countries.

REFERENCES

Adam, C. (1992) "On the dynamic specification of money demand in Kenya," *Journal of African Economies*, 1: 233-270.

Adam, C. (2000) "The transactions demand for money in Chile," *Economía Chilena*, 3: 33-53.

Alogoskoufis, G.S. and Smith, R.P (1991) 'The Phillips Curve, the persistence of inflation, and the Lucas critique: evidence from exchange-rate regimes," *American Economic Review*, 81: 1254–1275.

Akhtar, M.A. and Putnam, B.H. (1980) "Money demand and foreign exchange risk: The German case, 1972-1976," *Journal of Finance*, 35: 787-794.

Akinlo, A.E. (2005) "The stability of money demand in Nigeria: An autoregressive distributed lag approach," *Journal of Policy Modeling*, 28: 445-452.

Amano, R.A. and Wirjanto, T.S. (2000) "On the stability of long-run M2 demand in Japan," *The Japanese Economic Review*, 51: 536-543.

Angelini, P., Hendry, D.F. and Rinaldi, R. (1993) "An econometric analysis of money demand in Italy," available at http://ideas.repec.org/e/pan37.html.

Anglingkusumo, R. (2005) "Stability of the demand for real narrow money in Indonesia," Tinbergen Institute Discussion Paper TI 2005-051/4 (Jakarta: Tinbergen Institute).

Anoruo, E. (2002) "Stability of the Nigerian M2 money demand function in the SAP period," *Economics Bulletin*, 14: 1–9.

Arize, A.C, Darrat, A.F, and Meyer, D.J. (1990) "Capital mobility, monetization and money demand: evidence from Africa," *The American Economist*, XXXIV: 69-75.

Arize, A.C. and Shwiff, S.S. (1993) "Cointegration, real exchange rate and modelling the demand for broad money in Japan," *Applied Economics*, 25: 717-726.

Arnold, I.J.M. (2003) "A regional analysis of German money demand around reunification with implications for EMU," *Empirica*, 30: 63-80.

Arrau, P. and Gregorio, J.D. (1993) "Financial innovation and money demand: application to Chile and Mexico," *Review of Economics and Statistics*, 75: 524-530.

Asano, H. (1999) "Financial deregulation and stability of money demand: the Australian case," *Australian Economic Papers*, 38: 407-421.

Atkins, F. (2005) "Financial crises and money demand in Jamaica," Birkbeck working papers in Economics and Finance No. 0512 (London: University of London).

Baba, Y., Hendry, D.F. and Starr, R.M. (1992) "The demand for M1 in the U.S.A., 1960–1988," *Review of Economic Studies,* 59: 25–61.

Bahmani-Oskooee, M. (2001) "How stable is M2 money demand function in Japan?," *Japan and the World Economy*, 13: 455-461.

Bahmani-Oskooee, M. (2003) "The black market exchange rate and demand for money in Iran," *Journal of Macroeconomics*, 18: 171-176.

Bahmani-Oskooee, M. and Rehman, H., (2002) ``Stability of the money demand function in Asian developing countries," *Applied Economics*, 37: 773-792.

Bahmani-Oskooee, M. and Economidou, C. (2005) "How stable is the demand for money in Greece," *International Economic Journal*, 19: 461-472.

Ball, L. (1998) "Another look at long-run money demand," NBER Working Paper No. 6597 (New York: National Bureau of Economic Research, Inc.).

Baltensperger, E., Jordan, T.J. and Savioz, M.R. (2001) "The demand for M3 and inflation forecasts: An empirical analysis for Switzerland," *Review of World Economics*, 137: 244-272.

Baumol, W. (1952) 'The transactions demand for cash," *Quarterly Journal of Economics*, 67: 545-556.

Bhattacharya, B.B. (1974) "Demand and supply of money in a developing economy: a structural analysis for India," *The Review of Economics and Statistics*, 56: 502-510.

Brown, R.L., Durbin, J. and Evans, J.M. (1975) "Techniques for testing the constancy of regression relations over time," *Journal of the Royal Statistical Society*, 37: 149-192.

Bruggemann, I. and Nautz, D. (1997) "Money growth volatility and the demand for money in Germany: Friedmans volatility hypothesis revisited," *Review of World Economics*, 133: 523-537.

Bundesbank, D. (1995) "Demand for money and currency substitution in Europe," *Monthly Report,* 47: 33–49.

Bynoc, A.J. (2002) "Economic liberalization and money demand stability in Jamaica," *International Advances in Economic Research*, 8: 362.

Caporale, G.M. and Gil-Alana, L.A. (2005) "Fractional cointegration and aggregate money demand functions," *The Manchester School*, 73: 737-753.

Caruso, M. (2006) "Stock market fluctuations and money demand in Italy, 1913-2003," *Economic Notes*, 35: 1-47.

Cassard, M., Lane, T.D., and Masson, P.R. (1997) "Core ERM money demand and effects on inflation," *The Manchester School*, 65: 1-24.

Chaisrisawatsuk, S., Sharma, S.C. and Chowdhury, A.R. (2004) "Money demand stability under currency substitution: some recent evidence," *Applied Financial Economics*, 14: 19-27.

Charemza, W. and Deadman, D. (1997) "*New Directions in Econometric Practice,* 2nd Edition," Cheltonham: Edward Elgar.

Choi, D. and Oxley, L. (2004) "Modelling the demand for money in New Zealand," *Mathematics and Computers in Simulation*, 64: 185-191.

Chowdhury, A.R. (1995) "The demand for money in a small open economy: the case of Switzerland," *Open Economies Review,* 6: 131–144.

Cuthbertson, K. and Galindo, L. (1999) "The demand for money in Mexico," *The Manchester School*, 67: 154-166.

Das, S. And Mandal, K. (2000) "Modeling money demand in India: testing weak, strong and super exogeneity," *Indian Economic Review*, 35: 1-19.

Davidson, J., Hendry, D., Srba, F., and Yeo, S. (1978) ``Econometric modeling of the aggregate time-series relationship between consumers' expenditure and income in the United Kingdom," *The Economic Journal,* 88: 661-692.

De Brouwer, G., Ng, I. and Subbaraman (1993) "The demand for money in Australia: new tests on an old topic," RBA Discussion Paper No. 9314 (Sydney: Reserve Bank of Australia).

Dekle, R. and Pradhan, M. (1997) "Financial liberalization and money demand in ASEAN countries: implications for monetary policy," IMF Working Paper 97/36 (Washington: International Monetary Fund).

Dooley, M.P. and Spinelli, F. (1989) "The early stages of financial innovation and money demand in France and Italy," *The Manchester school*, 57: 107-124.

Drake, L. (1996) "Relative prices in the UK personal sector money demand function," *The Economic Journal*, 106: 1209-1226.

Drake, L. and Chrystal, K.A. (1994) "Company-sector money demand: new evidence on the existence of a stable long-run relationship for the United Kingdom," *Journal of Money, Credit, and Banking,* 26: 479–494.

Ebrill, L. (1989) "Money demand in Canada," IMF Working Paper 89/77 (Washington DC: International Monetary Fund).

Enders, W. (2004) "*Applied Econometric Time Series*, 2nd edition," (Hoboken NJ: John Wiley).

Enders, W. and Siklos, P. L. (2001) "Cointegration and threshold adjustment," *Journal of Business and Economic Statistics*, 19: 166-176.

Escribano, A. (2004) "Non linear error correction: the case of money demand in the United Kingdom (1878-2000)," *Macroeconomic Dynamics*, 8: 76-116.

E-views 5.0. (2004) *A Quantitative Micro-Software.* Irvine, CA: U.S.A.

Ericsson, N. and MacKinnon, J. (2002) ``Distributions of error correction tests for cointegration," *Econometrics Journal*, 5: 285-318.

Ericsson, N. and Sharma, S. (1998) "Broad money demand and financial liberalization in Greece," *Empirical Economics,* 23: 417-436.

Ewing, B.T. and Payne, J.E. (1999) "Long-run money demand in Chile," *Journal of Economic Development*, 24: 177-190.

Fase, M.M.G. and Winder, C.C.A. (1990) "The demand for money in the Netherlands revisited," *De Economist*, 138: 276-301.

--------------------------------(1996) "Wealth and the demand for money: empirical evidence for the Netherlands and Belgium," *De Economist*, 144: 569-589.

Felmingham, B. and Zhang, Q. (2001) "The long run demand for broad money in Australia subject to regime shifts," *Australian Economic Papers*, 40: 146-55.

Fielding, D. (1994) "Money demand in four African countries," *Journal of Economics Studies*, 21: 17-51.

Friedman, M. (1956) "The quantity theory of money- a restatement" in studies in the quantity theory of money, M. Friedman, ed.," Chicago, IL: University of Chicago Press.

Friedman, M. and Schwartz, A. (1991) "Alternative approaches to analyzing economic data," *American Economic Review,* 81: 39-49.

Fujiki, H. (1999) "Japanese money demand: evidence from regional monthly data," *Japan and the World Economy*, 11: 375-393.

Fujiki, H. and Mulligan, C.B. (1996) "A structural analysis of money demand: cross-sectional evidence from Japan," *Bank of Japan Monetary and Economic Studies*, 14: 53-78.

Gerlach-Kristen, P. (2001) "The demand for money in Switzerland 1936-1995," *Schweizerische Zeitschrift für Volkswirtschaft und Statistik*, 137: 535-554.

Georgopoulos, G. (2000) "Estimating demand for money in Canada: Does including an own rate of return matter?," available at http://www.utsc.utoronto.ca/mgmt/research/working-papers/jessay16.pdf.

Ghartey, E.E. (1998) "Money demand in Jamaica: evidence from cointegration, error correction modelling, and exogeneity," *North American Journal of Economics and Finance*, 9: 33-43.

Gregory, A.W. and Hansen, B.E. (1992) "Residual-based tests for cointegration in models with regime shifts," RCER Working Papers 335 (University of Rochester - Center for Economic Research).

Gregory, A.W. and Hansen, B.E. (1996a) "Residual-based tests for cointegration in models with regime shifts," *Journal of Econometrics*, 70: 99-126.

-------------------------------------- (1996b) "Tests for cointegration in models with regime and trend shifts," *Oxford Bulletin of Economics and Statistics*, 58: 555-559.

Gibson, W.E. (1972) "Demand and supply functions for money in the United States: theory and measurement," *Econometrica*, 40: 361-370.

Hafer, R.W. and Jansen, D.W. (1991) "The demand for money in the United States: evidence from cointegration tests," *Journal of Money, Credit and Banking*, 23: 155-168.

Hafer, R. and Kutan, A. (2003) "Financial innovation and the demand for money: evidence from the Philippines," *International Economic Journal,* 81: 17-27.

Hamori, N. and Hamori, S. (1999) "Stability of the money demand in Germany," *Applied Economics Letters*, 6: 329-332.

Hayo, B. (2000) "The demand for money in Austria," *Empirical Economics*, 25: 581-603.

Haug, A.A. (1999) " Money demand functions: data span and tests," available at http://www.econ.canterbury.ac.nz/research/working_papers.shtml.

Haug, A.A (2006) "Canadian money demand functions: cointegration-rank stability," *The Manchester School*, 74: 214-230.

Haug, A. A. and Lucas, R.F. (1996) "Long-term money demand in Canada: in search of stability," *The Review of Economics and Statistics,* 78: 345–48.

Hendry, D. and Ericsson, N. (1991) "An econometric analysis for the U.K. money demand in monetary trends in the Unites States and the United

Kingdom by Milton Friedman and Anna J. Schwartz," *American Economic Review,* 81: 8-38.

Herwartz, H. and Reimers, H. (2003) "Seasonal cointegration analysis for German M3 money demand," *Applied Financial Economics*, 13: 71-78.

Herz, B. and Roeger, W. (1990) "Evaluating conflicting stability results in German money demand regression," *Review of World Economics*, 126: 691-708.

Hoffman, D.L. and Rasche, R.H. (1991) "Money demand in the U.S. and Japan: analysis of stability and the importance of transitory and permanent shocks," available at http://ideas.repec.org/e/pra180.html.

Hoffman, D.L. and Tahiri, C. (1994) "Money demand in Morocco: estimating long-run elasticities for a developing country," *Oxford Bulletin of Economics and Statistics*, 56: 305-24.

Hossain, A. (2006) "The income and interest rate elasticities of demand for money in Bangladesh: 1973-2003," *The ICFAI Journal of Monetary Economics*, IV: 73-96.

Hossain, A. (1993) "Financial reforms, stability of the money demand function and monetary policy in Bangladesh: an econometric investigation," *Indian Economic Review*, 28: 85-100.

Hussain, Z., Awan, H., Hussain, I., Farhan, M., and Haq, I. (2006) "Demand for money in Pakistan," *International Research Journal of Finance and Economics*, 5: 209-218.

Hussain, H. and Liew, V.K. (2006) "Money demand in Malaysia: further empirical evidence," *The ICFAI Journal of Applied Economics*, V: 17-27.

International Financial Statistics, December, 2003/5. IMF CD-ROM (Washington DC: International Monetary Fund).

James, G.A. (2005) "Money demand and financial liberalization in Indonesia," *Journal of Asian Economics*, 16: 817-829.

Jayaraman, T.K. and Ward, B.D. (2000) "Demand for money in Fiji: An econometric analysis," *Pacific Economic Bulletin*, 15: 81-93.

Johansen, S. (1988) "Statistical analysis of cointegrating vectors," *Journal of Economics Dynamics and Control,* 12: 231-254.

Juselius, K. (1998) "A structured VAR for Denmark under changing monetary regimes," *Journal of Business and Economic Statistics*, 16: 400-411.

Kamath, S.J. (1985) "An investigation of the demand for and supply of money in India, 1951-1976," *Review of World Economics*, 121: 501-523.

Kannapiran, C. (2001) "Stability of money demand and monetary policy in Papua New Guinea: an error correction model analysis," *International Economic Journal*, 15: 73-84.

Karfakis, C. and Opoulos, M.S. (2000) "On the stability of the long-run money demand in Greece," *Applied Economics Letters*, 7: 83-86.

Katafono, R. (2001) "Demand for money in Fiji," Staff Working paper 03/2001 (Suva: The Reserve Bank of Fiji).

Khalid, A.M. (1999) "Modelling money demand in open economies: the case of selected Asian countries," *Applied Economics*, 31: 1129–1135.

Khamis, M.Y. and Leone, A.M. (1999) "Can currency demand be stable under a financial crisis? The case of Mexico," IMF Working Paper 99/53 (Washington: International Monetary Fund).

Kogar, C. (1995) "Cointegration test for money demand: the case for Turkey and Israel," available at http://www.econturk.org/Turkisheconomy/9514.pdf.

Komlos, J. (1987) "Financial innovation and the demand for money in Austria-Hungary, 1867-1913," *Journal of European Economic History*, 16: 587-606.

Krishnakumar, J. and Gueye, E. (1998) "An application of an error correction model with higher order cointegrated variables to the demand for money in Switzerland," available at http://www.inomics.com/cgi/repec?handle=RePEc:gen:geneem.

Kumar, S. (2007) 'The stability of demand for money in Bangladesh: time series methods,' *ICFAI Journal of Monetary Economics*, 5: pp.27-35.

Laidler, D. E. W. (1977) "The demand for money: theories and evidence 2nd edition," New York: Harper and Row.

Laidler, D.E.W. (1993) "The Demand for Money, 4th ed.," New York: Harper Collins College Publishers.

Lim, L.K. (1995) "Cointegration and an error correction model of money demand for Australia," *Mathematics and Computers in Simulation*, 39: 293-297.

Loizos, K. and Thompson, J. (2001) "The demand for money in Greece 1962 to1998," Center for International Banking, Economics and Finance Working Paper No.2/01 (Liverpool: Liverpool John Moores University).

Lucas, R.E. (1988) "Money demand in the United States: A quantitative review," *Carnegie-Rochester Conference Series on Public Policy*, 29: 137–168.

Lucas, R.E. and Haug, A.A. (1992) "Long-run money demand in Canada: in search of stability," available at http://ideas.repec.org/p/fth/saskat/92-4.html.

Luckett, D. (1987) "A preliminary study of the demand for money in Fiji," *Reserve Bank of Fiji, Quarterly Review, June, 1987* (Suva: Reserve bank of Fiji).

Lutkepohl, H., Teräsvirta, T. and Wolters, J. (1998) "Investigating stability and linearity of a German M1 money demand function," *Journal of Applied Econometrics*, 14: 511-525.

Lütkepohl, H. and Wolters, J. (1998) "A money demand system for German M3," *Empirical Economics*, 23, 371-386.

MacKinnon, J.G. (1991) "Critical values for cointegration tests' in Engle, R.F. and Granger, C.W.J. (eds) Long-run economic relationships: readings in cointegration," (Oxford: Oxford University Press).

Majid, M.A. (2004) "Reassessing the stability of broad money demand in Malaysia," available at http://ideas.repec.org/p/wpa/wuwpma/0405020.html.

Maki, D. and Kitasaka, S. (2006) "The equilibrium relationship among money, income, prices, and interest rates: evidence from a threshold cointegration test," *Applied Economics*, 38: 1585-1592.

Marashdeh, O. (1998) "The demand for money in an open economy: the case of Malaysia," available at http://129.3.20.41/eps/if/papers/9801/9801001.pdf.

Mark, N.C. and Sul, D. (2003) "Cointegration vector estimation by panel DOLS and long-run money demand," *Oxford Bulletin of Economics and Statistics*, 65: 665-680.

McNelis, P.D. (1998) "Money demand, financial distress, and exchange-rate uncertainty in Indonesia (1998)," available at http://citeseer.ist.psu.edu/278858.html.

McNown, R. and Wallace, M.S. (1992) "Cointegration tests of a long-run relation between money demand and the effective exchange rate," *Journal of International money and Finance*, 11: 107-114.

McPhail, K. (1991) "The long-run demand for money, Canada savings bonds and treasury bills in Canada," available at http://www.esri.go.jp/en/archive/dis/discussion-e.html.

Melnick, R. (1995) "Financial services, cointegration, and the demand for money in Israel," *Journal of Money, Credit and Banking*, 27: 140-153.

Miyagawa, S. and Morita, Y. (2004) "The recent monetary policy and money demand in Japan," Department of Economics Discussion Papers 04-15 (Denmark: University of Copenhagen).

Miyao, R. (1996) "Does a cointegrating M2 demand relation really exist in the United States?," *Journal of Money, Credit & Banking*, 28: 365-380.

Moosa, I. A. (1992) "The demand for money in India: a cointegration approach," *Indian Economic Journal,* 40: 101–15.

Moradi, M.A. (1999) "A microfoundation model of money demand in Iran: a cash-in-advance framework," Department of Economics and Accounting Working Paper No. 08/99 (Liverpool: University of Liverpool).

Nachega, J. (2001) "A cointegration analysis of broad money demand in Cameroon," IMF Working Paper 01/26 (Washington DC: International Monetary Fund).

Nagayasu, J. (2003) "A re examination of the Japanese money demand function and structural shifts," *Journal of Policy Modeling*, 25: 359-375.

Narayan, P.K. (2007) "Is money targeting an option for Bank Indonesia?," *Journal of Asian Economics*, 18: 726-738.

Nell, K.S. (1999) "The stability of money demand in South Africa, 1965-1997," available at http://www.inomics.net/cgi/repec?handle=RePEc: ukc:ukcedp.

Nell, K.S. (2003) "The stability of M3 money demand and monetary growth targets: the case of South Africa," *Journal of Development Studies*, 39: 155-180.

Nelson, C.R. and Plosser, C.I. (1982) "Trend's and random walks in macroeconomic time series: some evidence and implications," *Journal of Monetary Economics*, 10: 139-162.

Nielsen, H. (2004) "UK money demand 1873-2001: a cointegrated VAR analysis with additive data corrections," *Cliometrica*, 1: 45-61.

Nielsen, H., Tullio, G. and Wolters, J. (2004) "Currency substitution and the stability of the Italian demand for money before the entry into the monetary union, 1972–1998," *International Economics and Economic Policy*, 1: 73-85.

Nwaobi, G. (2001) "A vector error correction and nonnested modelling of money demand function in Nigeria," *Economics Bulletin*, 3: 1-8.

Orden, D. and Fisher, L.A. (1993) "Financial deregulation and the dynamics of money, prices, and output in New Zealand and Australia," *Journal of Money, Credit, and Banking,* 25: 273–92.

Owoye, O. and Onafowora, O.A. (2007) "M2 targeting, money demand, and real GDP growth in Nigeria: do rules apply?," *Journal of Business and Public Affairs*, 1: 1-20.

Papadopoulos, A.P. and Zis, G. (1997) "The demand for money in Greece: further empirical results and policy implications," *The Manchester School*, 65: 71-89.

Pedroni, P. (2004) "Panel cointegration: asymptotic and finite sample properties of pooled time series tests with an application to the PPP hypothesis", *Econometric Theory,* 3: 579–625.

Pesaran, M., and Pesaran, B. (1997) *Working with Microfit 4.0.* Oxford: Oxford University Press.

Peytrignet, M. and Stahel, C. (1998) "Stability of money demand in Switzerland: A comparison of the M2 and M3 cases," *Empirical Economics*, 23: 437-454.

Phillips, P., and Hansen, B. (1990) "Statistical inferences in instrumental variables regression with I(1) processes," *Review of Economic Studies,* 57: 99-125.

Poole, W. (1970) "The optimal choice of monetary policy instruments in a simple macro model," *Quarterly Journal of Economics*, 84: 197-216.

Pradhan, B., and Subaramanian, A. (2003) "On the stability of the demand for money in a developing economy: Some empirical issues," *Journal of Development Economics,* 72: 335-351.

Price, S. and Insukindro (1994) "The demand for Indonesian narrow money: long-run equilibrium, error correction and forward-looking behaviour," *Journal of InternationalTrade and Economic Development,* 3: 147–63.

Price, S. and Nasim, A. (1999) "Modelling inflation and the demand for money in Pakistan; cointegration and the causal structure," *Economic Modelling*, 16: 87-103.

Qayyum, A. (2005) "Modelling the demand for money in Pakistan," *The Pakistan Development Review*, 44: 233-252.

Ram, R. (1982) "Recent instability of the demand for money: another test of stability," *Southern Economic Journal*, 48: 1083-1087.

Ramachandran, M. (2004) "Do broad money, output, and prices stand for a stable relationship in India?," *Journal of Policy Modeling*, 26: 983-1001.

Rao, B.B (2007) Cointegration for the applied economist, 2nd Edition, Hampshire: Macmillan Publishers Limited.

Rao, B. B., (2006) "Estimating short and long run relationships: A guide to applied economists," forthcoming in *Applied Economics.*

Rao, B.B and Kumar, S (2007a) "Structural breaks, demand for money and Monetary policy in Fiji," *Pacific Economic Bulletin*, 22: 54-62.

Rao, B.B and Kumar, S (2007b) "Cointegration, structural breaks and demand for money in Bangladesh," forthcoming in *Applied Economics.*

Rao, B.B. and Shalabh (1995) "Unit roots cointegration and the demand for money in India," *Applied Economics Letters*, 2: 397-399.

Rao, B. and Singh, R. (2005a) “Cointegration and error correction approach to the demand for money in Fiji," *Pacific Economic Bulletin,* 20: 72-86.

--------------------- (2005b) “Demand for money in Fiji with PcGets", forthcoming in *Applied Economics Letters.*

---------------------- (2005c) “Demand for money in India: 1953-2003,” *Applied Economics*, 38: 1319-1326.

Serletis, A. (1987) “On the demand for money in the United States,” *Empirical Economics*, 12: 249-255.

Serletis, A. (2001) “The demand for money- theoretical and empirical approaches,” 1st Edition, Massachusetts: Kluwer Academic Publishers.

Shekar, B. and Hafizur, R. (1996) “The demand for money in Canada: a cointegration analysis,” *International Economic Journal*, 10: 29-45.

Siddiki, J.U. (2000) “Demand for money in Bangladesh: a cointegration analysis,” *Applied Economics*, 32: 977-1984.

Singh, R. and Kumar, S. (2010) “Some empirical evidence on the demand for money in the Pacific Island Countries,” *Studies in Economics and Finance*, 27, 211-222.

Singh, R. and Kumar, S. (2012) “Application of the alternative techniques to estimate demand for money in developing countries,” *Journal of Developing Areas*, 46, 43-63.

Smith, R. (2000) “Unit roots and all that: The impact of times series methods on macroeconomics," in Backhouse, R. and Salanti, A. (eds). *Macroeconomics and the Real World*, Oxford: Oxford University Press.

Soto, R. and Tapia, M. (2001) “Seasonal cointegration and the stability of the demand for money,” available at http://ideas.repec.org/e/pta57.html.

Sriram, S. S. (1999) “Survey of literature on demand for money: theoretical and empirical work with special reference to error-correction models," IMF Working Paper 7WP/99/64 (Washington DC: International Monetary Fund).

Stock, J.H. (1987) “Asymptotic properties of least squares estimators of cointegrating vectors,” *Econometrica*, 55, 1035-1056.

Sumner, M. (2008) “Demand for money in Thailand”, forthcoming in *Applied Economics.*

Swamy, P.A.V.B. (1987) “Financial deregulation, the demand for money, and monetary policy in Australia,” IMF Working Paper 87/74 (Washington DC: International Monetary Fund).

Taylor, M.P. (1994) “On the reinterpretation of money demand regressions,” *Journal of Money, Credit and Banking*, 26: 851-866.

Teriba, A. (2006) “Demand for M1 in Nigeria,” available at http://ssrn.com/abstract=874407.

The Asian Development Bank, (2005) ``Fiji's economic and financial Update - 2005," Key Indicators of Developing Asia and Pacific Countries. Manilla: The Asian Development Bank.

Thornton, J. (1996) “Cointegration, error correction, and the demand for money in Mexico,” *Review of World Economics*, 132: 690-699.

Tlelima, T. and Turner, P. (2004) “The demand for money in South Africa. Specification and tests for instability,” *The South African Journal of Economics*, 72: 25–36.

Tobin , J. (1956) “The Interest elasticity of the transactions demand for cash," *Review of Economics and Statistics*, 38: 241-247.

Traa, B. (1991) “Money demand in the Netherlands,” IMF Working Paper 91/57 (Washington DC: International Monetary Fund).

Turner, P. and Benavides, G. (2001) “The demand for money and inflation in Mexico 1980–1999: implications for stability and real seigniorage revenues,” *Applied Economics Letters*, 8: 775-778.

Valadkhani, A. (2003) “Long and short-run determinants of money demand in New Zealand: evidence from cointegration analysis,” School of Economics and Finance Discussion Paper No. 132 (Queensland: Queensland University of Technology).

Valadkhani, A. (2005) “Modelling demand for broad money in Australia,” *Australian Economic Papers*, 44: 47-64.

Valadkhani, A. and Alauddin, M. (2003) “Demand for M2 in developing countries: an empirical panel investigation,” School of Economics and Finance Discussion Paper No. 149 (Queensland: Queensland University of Technology).

Wesso, G. R. (2002) “Broad money demand and financial liberalization in South Africa,” Occasional Paper 18 (Pretoria: South African Reserve Bank).

White, W.R. (1979) “The demand for money in Canada and the control of monetary aggregates: evidence from the monthly data,” *Journal of Money, Credit and Banking*, 11: 127-129.

Yashiv, E. (1994) “Money demand in a high inflation economy: the case of Israel,” *Review of Economic and Statistics*, 76: 186-191.

Yildirim, J. (2003) "Currency substitution and the demand for money in five European Union countries," *Journal of Applied Economics*, 6: 361-383.

Yossifov, P.K. (1998) "Estimation of a money demand function for M2 in the U.S.A. in a vector error correction model," Phd Dissertation in Economics (Delaware: University of Delaware).

Ziegelschmidt, H. (1985) "The demand for money in Austria: Is it stable?," *Empirica*, 12: 3-24.

Zivot, E. and Andrews, D.W.K. (1992) "Further evidence on great crash, the oil price shock and the unit root hypothesis," *Journal of Business and Economic Statistics*, 10: 251-270.

APPENDICES

A. DEFINITION OF VARIABLES

P = GDP deflator (2000=100). Data derived are from International Financial Statistics (IFS-2005) and Asian Development Bank (ADB) database (2005).

Y = Nominal GDP at factor cost or market prices, whichever is available. Data are from IFS-2005 and ADB database (2005).

R = The average short-term (maximum of 3 years) savings deposit rate. Data derived from the IFS-2005 and ADB database (2005).

M = Currency in circulation, including demand deposit and bills payable. Seasonally adjusted data obtained from IFS-2005 and ADB database (2005).

Notes:

1. All variables, except the rate of interest, are deflated with the GDP deflator and are in natural logs.

B. Unit Root Tests

Table B(i). ADF Unit Root Tests

	Lags	$ln\ M_t$	$\Delta ln\ M_t$	$ln\ Y_t$	$\Delta ln\ Y_t$	R_t	ΔR_t
FJI	[2,1,1,0,3,0]	2.354	5.908	1.422	9.073	0.777	6.328
VNT	[0,0,1,0,1,1]	1.172	5.667	1.171	3.844	1.158	6.555
SAM	[1,1,1,0,1,0]	1.479	3.756	2.186	4.218	1.378	4.472
SOL	[0,0,1,0,2,0]	1.403	5.228	1.503	3.324	1.222	4.098
TNG	[1,1,0,2,1,0]	1.239	6.780	2.003	3.868	2.211	4.328
IND	[0,2,1,0,1,3]	0.790	5.792	0.346	8.914	0.293	3.711
BGD	[1,1,0,2,1,1]	0.923	4.573	1.902	3.772	2.235	3.870
PHL	[0,0,1,1,3,3]	2.370	5.869	2.573	3.964	2.746	3.638
IDN	[2,1,2,1,2,0]	2.612	7.081	0.053	5.747	1.739	5.500
THA	[0,1,1,1,3,1]	1.311	5.245	1.679	4.618	1.653	4.020
JAM	[0,0,1,0,0,0]	1.778	6.407	2.563	3.618	1.467	7.945
KEN	[0,0,1,3,3,1]	1.519	7.976	2.239	6.075	0.360	4.313
RWA	[0,0,0,0,3,3]	2.032	4.611	1.964	4.772	0.826	3.904
MWI	[1,2,0,0,0,0]	1.254	3.756	2.598	7.328	2.263	3.719
ZAF	[0,1,1,0,2,2]	2.304	3.721	1.223	6.894	1.662	5.837

Notes:

1. $ln\ M_t$ and $ln\ Y_t$ represent log of real money and real income, respectively.
2. The respective 1% and 5% critical values for ADF test are 3.685 and 2.970.
3. Lag lengths are for the respective variables selected with AIC and SBC criteria. For example [0,1] indicates that lag 0 and 1 are significant in 1st and 2nd columns, respectively.

C. JML Identification and Exogeneity Tests

Table C(i). JML Identification and Exogeinity Tests

	Fiji			Vanuatu		
	$\Delta ln\ M_t$	$\Delta ln\ Y_t$	ΔR_t	$\Delta ln\ M_t$	$\Delta ln\ Y_t$	ΔR_t
$ECMM_{t-1}$	-1.229 (8.28)*	-0.148 (1.56)	-1.353 (0.42)	-1.312 (6.39)*	3.255 (1.75)**	22.431 (1.10)
$ECMY_{t-1}$		0.012 (2.62)*			-0.008 (0.03)	
$ECMR_{t-1}$			0.002 (0.39)			0.074 (3.14)*
	Samoa			Solomons		
	$\Delta ln\ M_t$	$\Delta ln\ Y_t$	ΔR_t	$\Delta ln\ M_t$	$\Delta ln\ Y_t$	ΔR_t
$ECMM_{t-1}$	-0.857 (18.09)*	-0.105 (0.55)	-4.382 (1.53)	-0.483 (2.73)*	0.037 (0.82)	-1.874 (1.70)**
$ECMY_{t-1}$		0.105 (1.53)			-0.008 (0.186)	
$ECMR_{t-1}$			-0.489 (1.53)			-0.073 (1.40)
	India			Philippines		
	$\Delta ln\ M_t$	$\Delta ln\ Y_t$	ΔR_t	$\Delta ln\ M_t$	$\Delta ln\ Y_t$	ΔR_t
$ECMM_{t-1}$	-0.388 (2.35)*	0.219 (1.07)	-3.502 (0.54)	-1.120 (3.48)*	-0.159 (1.03)	-4.488 (0.85)
$ECMY_{t-1}$		-0.247 (1.07)			0.213 (1.09)	
$ECMR_{t-1}$			-0.079 (0.543)			-0.211 (0.88)
	Tonga			Bangladesh		
	$\Delta ln\ M_t$	$\Delta ln\ Y_t$	ΔR_t	$\Delta ln\ M_t$	$\Delta ln\ Y_t$	ΔR_t
$ECMM_{t-1}$	-0.141 (4.05)*	0.478 (1.38)	1.230 (1.02)	-0.208 (3.28)*	-2.678 (1.23)	-1.148 (0.45)
$ECMY_{t-1}$		0.119 (0.45)			1.292 (0.29)	
$ECMR_{t-1}$			-0.147 (0.25)			-0.321 (0.86)

Notes:

1. Absolute *t*-ratios are reported below the coefficients. Significance at 5% & 10% are indicated by * and **, respectively.
2. $ln\ M_t$ and $ln\ Y_t$ represent log of real money and real income, respectively.
3. $ECMM_{t-1}$, $ECMY_{t-1}$ and $ECMR_{t-1}$ are the lagged residuals of the CVs normalized on money, income, and rate of interest, respectively for each country.
4. Although $ECMR_{t-1}$ is strongly significant in ΔR_t equation for Vanuatu, the sign is incorrect.

Table C(ii). JML Identification and Exogeneity Tests

	Indonesia			Thailand		
	$\Delta ln\ M_t$	$\Delta ln\ Y_t$	ΔR_t	$\Delta ln\ M_t$	$\Delta ln\ Y_t$	ΔR_t
$ECMM_{t-1}$	-0.439 (2.26)*	-0.235 (1.72)**	-9.500 (0.52)	-0.552 (2.02)*	-0.049 (0.48)	-3.612 (0.82)
$ECMY_{t-1}$		-0.260 (1.72)**			-0.140 (0.82)	
$ECMR_{t-1}$			-0.121 (0.52)			-0.140 (0.82)
	Jamaica			Kenya		
	$\Delta ln\ M_t$	$\Delta ln\ Y_t$	ΔR_t	$\Delta ln\ M_t$	$\Delta ln\ Y_t$	ΔR_t
$ECMM_{t-1}$	-0.831 (3.66)*	0.067 (0.87)	-7.480 (0.59)	-0.113 (2.05)*	0.073 (1.48)	-0.265 (0.21)
$ECMY_{t-1}$		-0.069 (0.87)			-0.093 (1.48)	
$ECMR_{t-1}$			-0.047 (0.59)			-0.027 (0.21)
	Rwanda			Malawi		
	$\Delta ln\ M_t$	$\Delta ln\ Y_t$	ΔR_t	$\Delta ln\ M_t$	$\Delta ln\ Y_t$	ΔR_t
$ECMM_{t-1}$	-0.353 (2.05)*	0.685 (1.84)**	5.057 (1.51)	-0.409 (2.88)*	-0.090 (1.37)	2.581 (0.33)
$ECMY_{t-1}$		-0.696 (1.84)**			-0.960 (1.37)	
$ECMR_{t-1}$			0.372 (1.51)			0.020 (0.33)
	South Africa					
	$\Delta ln\ M_t$	$\Delta ln\ Y_t$	ΔR_t			
$ECMM_{t-1}$	-0.324 (5.67)*	4.535 (1.33)	1.237 (1.51)			
$ECMY_{t-1}$		-0.627 (1.21)				
$ECMR_{t-1}$			-0.212 (0.27)			

Notes:

1. Absolute t-ratios are reported below the coefficients. Significance at 5% & 10% are indicated by * and **, respectively.
2. $ln\ M_t$ and $\ln Y_t$ represent log of real money and real income, respectively.
3. $ECMM_{t-1}$, $ECMY_{t-1}$ and $ECMR_{t-1}$ are the lagged residuals of the CVs normalized on money, income, and rate of interest, respectively for each country.
4. Although $ECMY_{t-1}$ is mildly significant in ΔlnY_t equation for Rwanda, it also has incorrect sign.

D. JML STABILITY TESTS

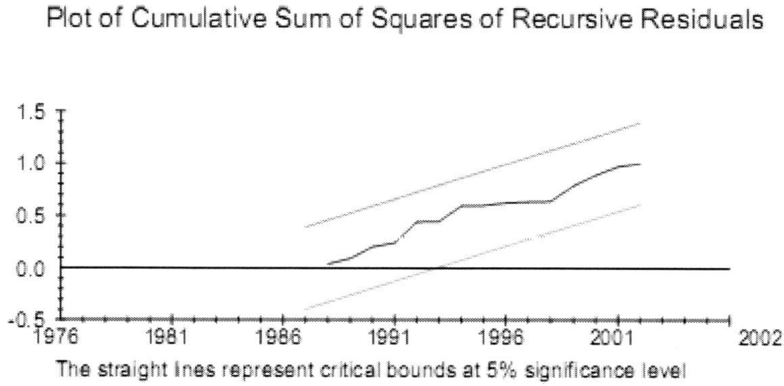

Figure 1. CUSUM SQUARES Test for FJI (JML).

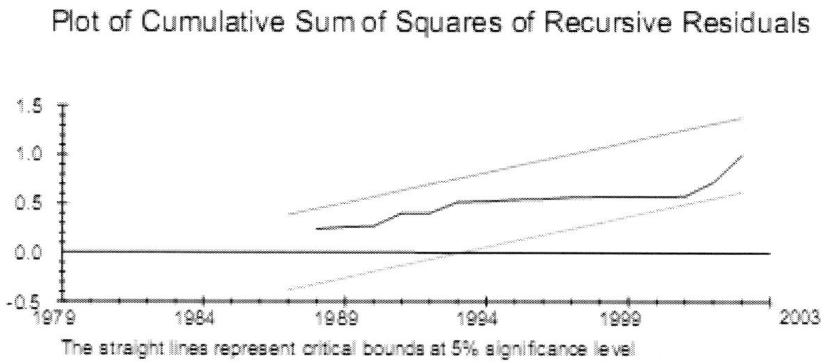

Figure 2. CUSUM SQUARES Test for VNT (JML).

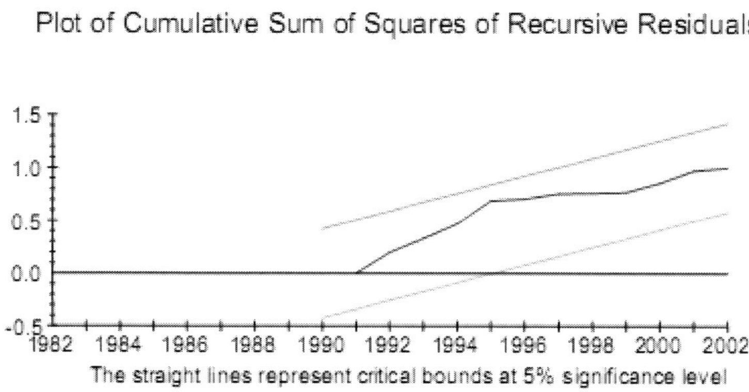

Figure 3. CUSUM SQUARES Test for SAM (JML).

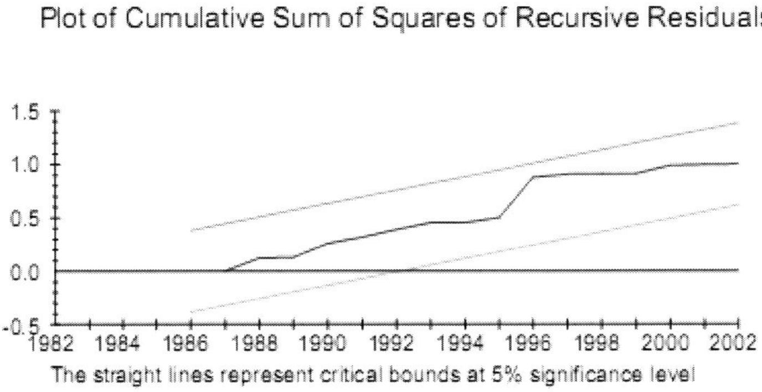

Figure 4. CUSUM SQUARES Test for SOL (JML).

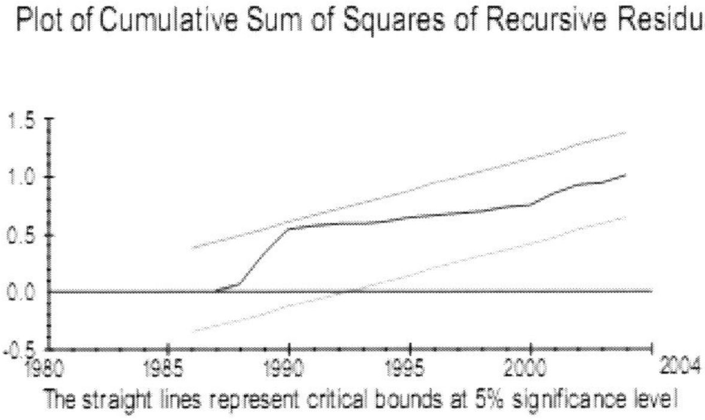

Figure 5. CUSUM SQUARES Test for TNG (JML).

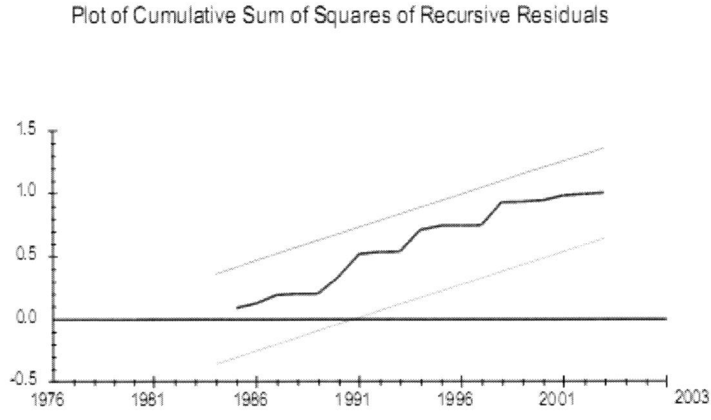

Figure 6. CUSUM SQUARES Test for BGD (JML).

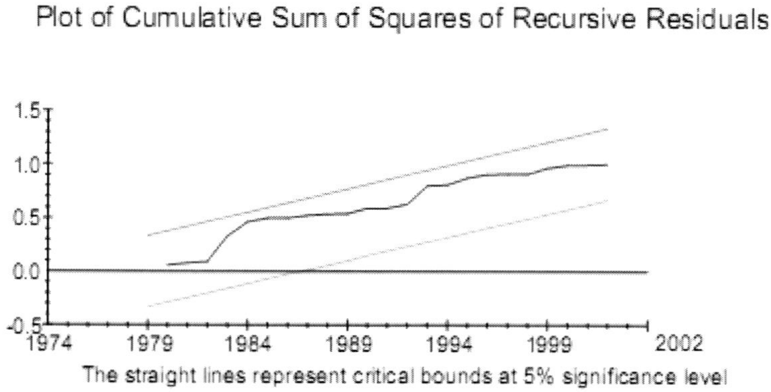

Figure 7. CUSUM SQUARES Test for IND (JML).

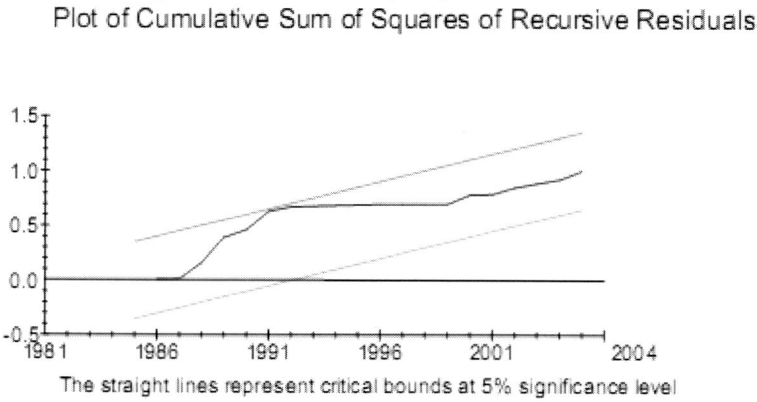

Figure 8. CUSUM SQUARES Test for PHL (JML).

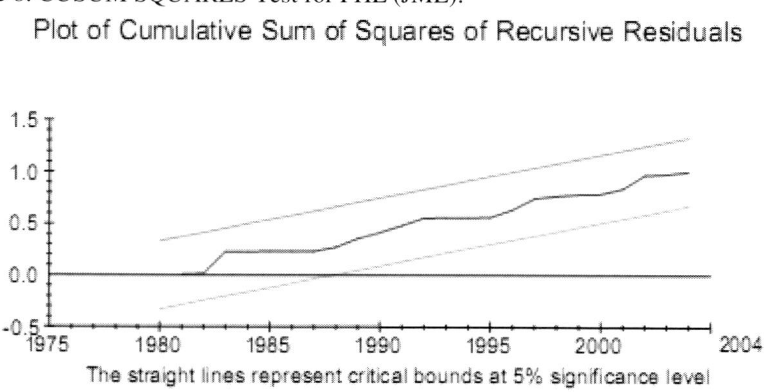

Figure 9. CUSUM SQUARES Test for IDN (JML).

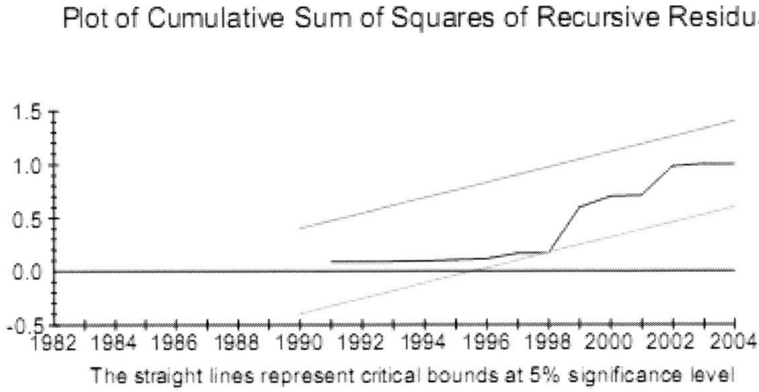

Figure 10. CUSUM SQUARES Test for THA (JML).

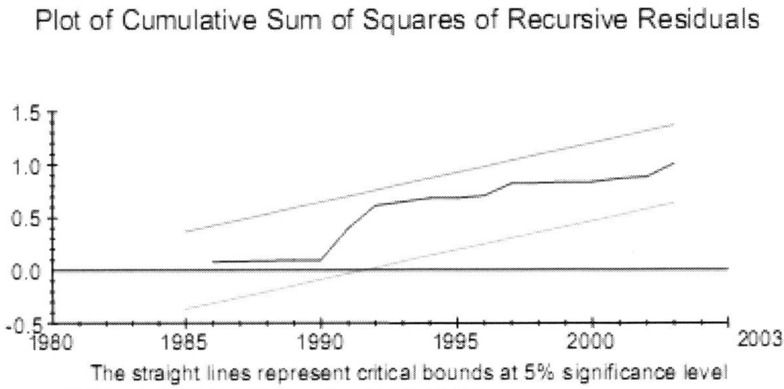

Figure 11. CUSUM SQUARES Test for JAM (JML).

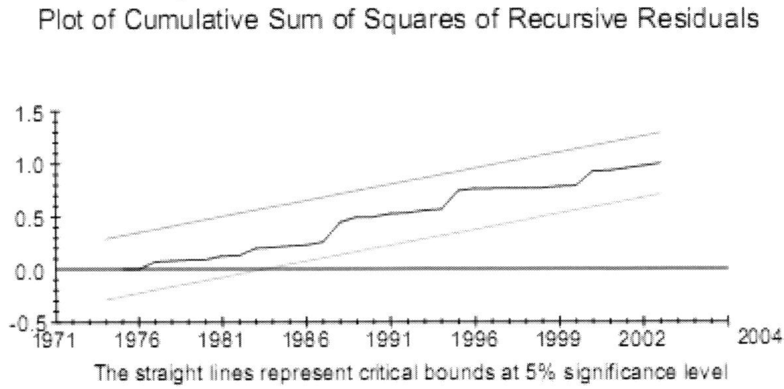

Figure 12. CUSUM SQUARES Test for KEN (JML).

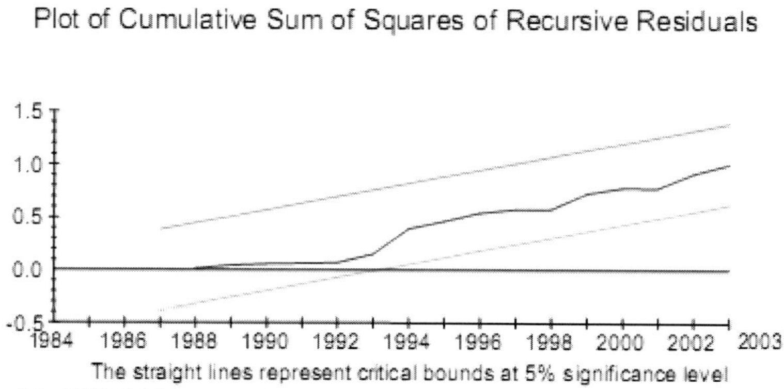

Figure 13. CUSUM SQUARES Test for RWA (JML).

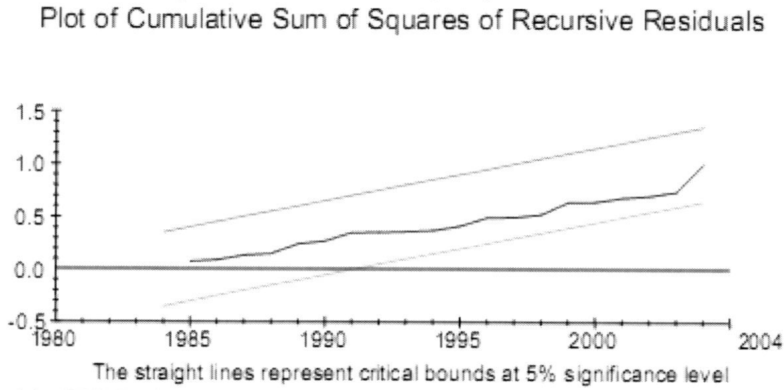

Figure 14. CUSUM SQUARES Test for MWI (JML).

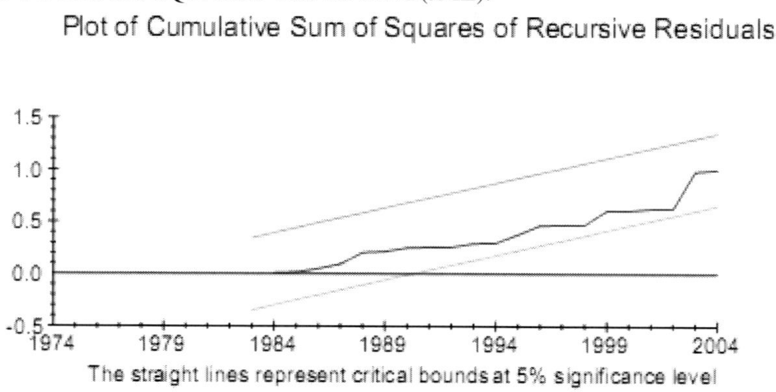

Figure 15. CUSUM SQUARES Test for ZAF (JML).

AUTHOR CONTACT INFORMATION

Dr. Saten Kumar
Lecturer in Economics
Department of Economics, Auckland
University of Technology
Private Mail Bag 92006
Auckland 1142, New Zealand
kumar_saten@yahoo.com

INDEX

A

B

C

D

E

F

G

I

J

K

L

M

N

P

Q

R

S

T

U

V

W